States and Nationalism in Europe since 1945

From the end of the Second World War until the recent break-up of the Communist regimes, there has been a widespread assumption that the age of nationalism has passed, and that nationalism was made up of a set of dangerous and disastrous ideas.

States and Nationalism examines the ceaseless controversies surrounding the ideas of the nation and nationalism, and shows that they are very far from dead in twenty-first century Europe. Beginning by defining these terms and setting out theories and concepts clearly and concisely, this book analyses the impact of nationalism since the Second World War, covering themes including:

- the relationship of nationalism to the Cold War
- the reemergence of demands by stateless nations
- European integration and globalisation and their effects
- immigration since the 1970s
- the effects of nationalism on the former Soviet Union, Eastern Europe and Yugoslavia

Malcolm Anderson is Professor Emeritus of the University of Edinburgh. His books include *Frontiers, Territory and State Formation in the Contemporary World* (Polity Press, 1996) and *Policing the World: Interpol and the Politics of International Police Cooperation* (Clarendon Press, 1989).

The Making of the Contemporary World
Edited by Eric Evans and Ruth Henig
University of Lancaster

The Making of the Contemporary World series provides challenging interpretations of contemporary issues and debates within strongly defined historical frameworks. The range of the series is global, with each volume drawing together material from a range of disciplines – including economics, politics and sociology. The books in this series present compact, indispensable introductions for students studying the modern world.

Titles include:

The Uniting of Europe
From discord to concord
Stanley Henig

International Economy Since 1945
Sidney Pollard

United Nations in the Contemporary World
David J. Whittaker

Latin America
John Ward

Thatcher and Thatcherism
Eric J. Evans

Decolonization
Raymond Betts

The Soviet Union in World Politics, 1945–1991
Geoffrey Roberts

China Under Communism
Alan Lawrance

The Cold War
An interdisciplinary history
David Painter

Conflict and Reconciliation in the Contemporary World
David J. Whittaker

Forthcoming titles include:

Multinationals
Peter Wardley

Pacific Asia
Yumei Zhang

Conflicts in the Middle East since 1945
Beverley Milton-Edwards and Peter Hinchcliffe

The Irish Question
Patrick Maume

Right Wing Extremism
Paul Hainsworth

Women into Power
Ruth Henig

US Foreign Policy since 1945
Alan Dobson and Steven Marsh

The Division and Unification of Germany
J. K. A. Thomaneck and William Niven

States and Nationalism in Europe since 1945

Malcolm Anderson

London and New York

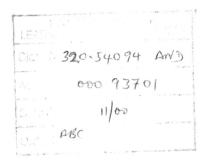
First published 2000
by Routledge
11 New Fetter Lane, London EC4P 4EE

Simultaneously published in the USA and Canada
by Routledge
29 West 35th Street, New York, NY 10001

Routledge is an imprint of the Taylor & Francis Group

© 2000 Malcolm Anderson

Typeset in Times New Roman by
HWA Text and Data Management Ltd
Printed and bound in Great Britain by
Biddles Ltd, Guildford and King's Lynn

British Library Cataloguing in Publication Data
A catalogue record for this book is available from the British
Library

Library of Congress Cataloging in Publication Data
Anderson, Malcolm.
  States and nationalism in Europe since 1945 / Malcolm
Anderson.
    p. cm. — (The making of the contemporary world)
  Includes bibliographical references and index.
    1. Europe—Politics and government—1945–
  2. Nationalism—Europe—History—20th century. I. Title.
  II. Series.

D1053 .A54 2000
320.54′094′09045—dc21   00-025486

ISBN 0–415–19558–6 (pbk)
ISBN 0–415–19557–8 (hbk)

Contents

Acknowledgements

I thank most warmly those who have taken the trouble to read the whole of this book in draft – Desmond King, Jacqueline Larrieu and Neil MacCormick – and those who read substantial parts of it – Eberhard Bort and Nigel Bowles. I also owe a debt of gratitude to Pierre Birnbaum, whose major edited volume (1997) *Sociologie des Nationalismes*, Presses Universitaires Françaises, is unfortunately not available in English.

Introduction

This book is concerned with the impact of nationalism in Europe since the end of the Second World War. Most of the vast literature on nationalism is concerned with the two questions – what is a nation or national identity, and what is nationalism? This short introduction is more concerned with the effects of nationalism in the making of contemporary Europe. Although nationalism is a world-wide phenomenon, it is impractical in this short book to attempt a global coverage. Moreover, nationalism originated in Europe, some of its most troublesome manifestations are present in Europe, and the most influential challenges to nationalist assumptions have recently occurred in Europe.

We should start with a preliminary definition of nationalism. Nationalism is an expression of certain straightforward ideas which provide a framework for political life. These ideas are non-negotiable precepts and not a fully worked out political philosophy. Basic ideas are that most people belong to a national group which is reasonably homogeneous. These nations have characteristics – habits, ways of thinking and institutions – which clearly distinguish them from other national groups; that nations should be 'self-determining' and preferably have independent governments; that 'our nation' is somehow better than other nations, although it may sometimes be grouped with other 'like-minded nations'. Most leading politicians in Europe, since the Second World War, have been touched by some or all of these attitudes, without thinking of themselves as nationalists. Also for large numbers of ordinary citizens, these attitudes are not identified as nationalism but, to adapt the words of Mrs Thatcher, have been 'plain common sense'.

THE DURABILITY OF NATIONALISM

A widespread assumption from the end of the Second World War until the disintegration of the communist regimes was that the great age of nationalism had passed, and many thought that nationalism incarnated a set of obsolescent, dangerous and objectionable ideas. The overwhelming influence of nationalism in the nineteenth and first half of the twentieth centuries seemed self-evidently disastrous, and European societies, it was assumed, had developed 'post-national' attitudes. Nationalism, which had seemed progressive and liberating in the nineteenth century, had become associated with political disaster, and with unacceptable attitudes and behaviour. The term re-acquired the meaning given to it by the Jesuit Abbé Barruel (who is credited with inventing the expression), at the end of the eighteenth century, as scorn and antagonism towards foreigners.

But states and nationalism have been intertwined in modern European history and have recently spread to the whole of the inhabited world. States have derived their legitimacy from the national principle. Some multinational states were undermined by national sentiments and some disintegrated. Nationalism, as part of a universal ideal, apparently triumphed at the end of the First World War when national self-determination was accepted in principle, if not always in practice, for allocating territory in the peace settlements. The degeneration of nationalism into its extreme forms in fascism and nazism, and their defeat in the Second World War, apparently discredited it. But it was very far from dead and persisted in popular attitudes, and in appeals made by politicians for support. In some respects, the social democratic consensus of post-war West Europe strengthened a sense of identification with nations because of the material benefits which the nation-state provided. More recently, virulent nationalism, whose emblematic figures are Milosovec in Serbia and Zhirinovsky in Russia, has been going through a revival in East Europe since the collapse of Soviet Communism.

CONTROVERSIES ABOUT NATIONALISM

The ideas of the nation and nationalism continue to be the subject of endless controversies. There is now some common ground between the various schools of thought. It is generally accepted that nationalism is easier to define than the nation. Nationalism is almost universally regarded as a political doctrine whose core tenet is that the nation is the source of sovereignty and political legitimacy. Nationalists also believe that the boundaries of a state should coincide with the boundaries of a nation. The idea of a nation is thus associated with a place, a 'homeland' which a nation occupies by right. The nation is the primary identity of individuals who may be divided by other things such as social class, religion and family loyalty. Some nationalists admit that multinational states are possible, even if a second best alternative to the nation-state, but they can only be legitimate if the nations which compose them fully consent to join them and they have the right to withdraw their consent.

There is also little dispute that nationalism is a modern political doctrine, with origins in the late eighteenth and early nineteenth centuries. Elie Kedourie in his celebrated opening sentence to his book on nationalism asserted: 'Nationalism is a doctrine invented in Europe at the beginning of the nineteenth century.'[1] However, national consciousness, national sentiment and nations often appear very much older. Some peoples, such as the Jews and the Chinese, well aware of their differences with other peoples, are as old as recorded history. Some argue that nations are very much older than nationalism, and have played a crucial role both in history before the end of the eighteenth century and in the invention of modern nationalism. According to this strand of thought, nations are age-old phenomena and nationalism merely represented a change in beliefs about the sources of political authority. Although there has been much myth making about the origins of nations, there are episodes when beginnings of a national sentiment have been forged. These have occurred during a struggle to repel invaders – the Saracens in Spain (from end of eighth to end of fifteenth centuries), the Mongols in Russia (thirteenth to fifteenth centuries), the English in France during the Hundred Years war (fourteenth to fifteenth centuries) are striking examples of episodes when precocious national sentiment developed.

Other writers on nationalism have, however, argued that nations, as we now understand them, arose contemporaneously with the doctrine of nationalism. They were a structural requirement of the transition to modernity, marked by urbanisation and industrialisation. The symbols, the modes of thought and the practical impact of nations were radically new. National identities were novel constructions, necessitated by social and geographical mobility, which undermined the old society of 'estates' (nobility, clergy, commoners) who owed personal allegiance to princes, and by new forms of economic organisation which required unified markets, widely understood languages and mobile work-forces. This controversy between the so-called 'modernists' and 'primordialists' has lost its clear, confrontational character.[2] Modernisers are now usually prepared to admit that pre-existing peoples with some of the characteristics of modern nations and national consciousness both were present prior to the late eighteenth century and were even necessary for the creation of modern nations. Primordialists are willing to accept that the economic and social change has profoundly modified nations and the national identity of large populations.

A second important division over the idea of the nation and its implications for political organisation became evident in the aftermath of the French Revolution. The two sides of this division have often been identified, in a highly over-simplified way, with French and German thinking.[3] For those in the French Republican tradition, a nation was a large group of people who identified with one another, who had shared experiences and who, as citizens of a state, had common rights and obligations. An influential German strand of thought suggested that nations are natural phenomena; individuals are born into nations and therefore share certain objective characteristics such as a common language. In this view of the nation there is an essential blood relationship. In the nineteenth and first half of the twentieth centuries, many thought that this blood relationship resulted in shared physical, psychological and social characteristics. This contrasted with the 'French' view which suggests that the nation is a politically created association of a group of people who form, or who aspire to form, a state; there is a certain liberty for individuals to join the nation or to leave it.

Both these contrasting views remain influential, especially in controversies over citizenship. For some, they represent the two faces of nationalism, on the one side civic nationalism and on the other ethnic nationalism and that many people believe in both, at the same or at different times, despite their apparent contradiction. This also leads to the 'Janus faced' quality of nationalism, identified by Tom Nairn and Dominique Schnapper, which can sometimes seem a necessary support for social solidarity, democracy and self-government but can also seem to incite hostility towards other peoples, exclusion and discrimination, conflicts and wars.[4] However, there has been a growing tendency, expressed by Dominique Schnapper, to regard the contrast between the two views as misleading and that 'really existing' nations are an amalgam of historically based human societies, and a political project. Nations should, according to this way of thinking, be seen as based on a blood tie as well as on a political foundation.

CHARACTERISTICS OF NATIONALISM

Nationalism may be a global phenomenon but it has many forms and each form has its own special history although there may be some similarities between the societies whose individuals come to regard themselves as a nation which has the right to self rule. This is the theme of Liah Greenfield's impressive study of five cases of nationalism which her sub-title refers to as five roads to modernity.[5] She takes the examples of England, which she regards historically as the first nation, France, often regarded by others as the first modern nation, Russia, Germany and the United States, and shows that the development of these nations and the content of their national consciousness is very different. National identities and national consciousness may therefore share very little in common except as expressions of a basic framework for political and social order.

However, nationalism elevates everyone within a particular community, small or large, to the status of a member of the nation – in this sense it is a powerful integrating ideology, the most powerful to have emerged in modern history. It stands in contrast to the societies of orders, estates or castes, which it replaced. Membership of a nation also means being a member of an elite group, in some important respects superior to other peoples or nations. Members of nations that are weak in a political, economic or demographic sense pretend to superior cultural or spiritual values. This sense of superiority gave to nationalism a quality previously characterising religions – people were prepared to make the supreme sacrifice of their lives in order to defend or promote the superior cause of the 'nation'.

Nationalism is not always represented by forms of particularism but may be express universalism. In other words, to be Catalan is a highly particularist identity of a people living in a defined and restricted area, carriers of a specific cultural identity and speaking a language which is very little spoken outside the area. Other nations, such as the French, the American and the Russian, may regard themselves as having a universal mission and as carriers of universal truths. Both types of nationalism may either be expressed in aggressive attitudes or in defensive ones. American isolationists regarded 'the American way' as superior to others and of universal application no less than those who agree with the ringing espousal of global responsibilities in the 1961 Presidential acceptance speech of John F. Kennedy. French universalism may have been expressed by the aggressive conquests of the Revolutionary armies and Napoleon. But this aggressiveness was matched and surpassed by the particularist German nationalism from the mid-nineteenth to the mid-twentieth centuries.

NATIONALISM AND SPECIAL INTERESTS

All nations are, in the senses described above, 'imagined communities', to invoke the much-used term invented by Benedict Anderson.[6] Nations exist in the imaginations of large numbers of individuals, who do not know one another. National loyalty is apparently disinterested and self-sacrificing. It mobilises large masses of people in a 'higher' cause. But questions have been repeatedly raised about whether nationalism is a cover for particular interests – whether the imagining of nations has been to promote, consciously or unconsciously, the interests of particular groups or classes within these nations. The wars, the slaughter and the massacres culminating in the supreme ghastliness of the Holocaust during the Second World War have made these arguments persuasive. The obvious profit derived by powerful and unpopular interests, such as arms manufacturers, by their support of nationalist causes was grist to the mill of those, like Dr Johnson in the eighteenth century, who have believed that 'patriotism is the last refuge of the scoundrel'.

Moreover, nations have been 'imagined' in different ways, and some seemed designed to promote particular causes. For the French Revolutionaries at the end of the eighteenth century, the idea of sovereignty of the nation was conceived as a universal truth but it clearly hostile to an *ancien régime* and to all traditionally-established and divinely-ordained political authority. It promoted the interests of a rising class of republican politicians who could count on the support of social groups with material benefits to gain from political change. A more recent French illustration is De Gaulle's idea of France elegantly expressed in the first two pages of his war memoirs. This is an excellent example of the Hegelian 'spirit of the nation', made up of images and historical memories. This approach to the nation divorces it from what the majority of the French people actually believed or, in practice, did in specific circumstances. It provided the intellectual framework for the Gaullist-led national resistance to Nazi occupation even though the resistance movement mobilised only a small minority of the French people. De Gaulle claimed to represent the legitimacy of France, and events provided a justification for this claim.

John Plamenatz identified an 'eastern European' nationalism which he thought of as a political project to create nations where they previously did not exist or existed only in the minds of a certain intelligentsia.[7] Nationalist activists sought to create the cultural bases of nationhood, to raise vernacular speech into national languages, create a national literature and to write histories for peoples who were described by Marx as *geschichtlos*, peoples without history. The nationalists then proceeded to create states on the basis of this newly created cultural consciousness. Given the ethnic mix of Eastern Europe, Plamenatz rightly thought that this was a recipe for catastrophe. But the aim of nationalist activists in Eastern Europe was to throw off alien rule, to create self-governing free peoples and to modernise their societies. This is very much the same project as nationalists of the former colonial possessions of the European powers during and after the de-colonisation period. But self-selected leaders of political nationalist movements where national cultures and nation-states do not exist (or exist only in embryonic form) are exposed to the charge that the principles and ideology on which they allegedly base their action are self-serving.

Opponents of nationalism have always tended to take for granted that nationalism serves class or group interests. Karl Marx famously regarded it as bourgeois ideology – that is to say a set of erroneous beliefs supporting the interests of the capitalist class. But Marx also held the view that large nation-states were the political form best suited to bourgeois rule, a necessary stage on the way to a socialist society, because they guaranteed the existence of large homogeneous markets. He therefore favoured some expressions of nationalism such as German and Italian unification, and the Polish national cause. Engels went further and supported the Irish nationalism as a means of subverting one of the great centres of capitalism, England. In the twentieth century most Marxists have supported national liberation movements in the less developed world and some have even championed the cause of the separatist movements in Europe on the grounds that this would weaken existing states, and with them, the capitalist order.

Nationalism has presented a serious problem for those in the Marxist tradition, as well as other left-wing opponents of nationalism. Many radicals have promoted ideas of internationalism, universal human rights and global solidarity. However, the appeal to national sentiment has always proven stronger, when life and death issues were posed, than appeals to any other solidarity, particularly international class solidarity. The first half of the twentieth century is littered with catastrophic examples of failures of internationalism. Among these are the collapse of the Second Socialist International at the outbreak of the First World War, the failure of the League of Nations to prevent aggression and the futility of attempts to create an effective international anti-fascist movement in the inter-war period. Part of the responsibility for these failures resides with the self-defeating activities of those who proclaimed the international solidarity of the working classes. But attempts by Marxists to explain both the compelling and enduring nature, and the effectiveness of appeals to national sentiment have not been persuasive. In more recent years, some left-wing thinkers, such as Tom Nairn, have concluded that nothing progressive can enduringly be achieved against the grain of national sentiment.

In 1990, the Marxist historian Eric Hobsbawm could write that we are witnessing the end of the era of nations. There were many to reject this view at that time and now few, even among those who are politically committed to transcending the nation-state in a European Union or in stronger global regimes, would agree with him. In the 1990s, the bitter, violent and intractable disputes in former Yugoslavia and in the former USSR (Union of Soviet Socialist Republics) have been associated either with the aggressive assertion of national rights or in defence of the very existence of the nation. Observers in Western Europe could, and did, adopt the view that these conflicts were symptomatic of the economic, social and political backwardness of these societies. However, in the present decade, nationalism has revived in the 'advanced' part of the continent in two forms. First, a new assertiveness of small nations like the Scots, the Catalans and, at a different level, the Danes, has developed. Second, hostility to a 'supranational' Europe has grown, even in countries like France and Germany which have long been the motors of European integration. It is no longer possible to dismiss nationalism as an aberration of backward societies.

THE MAIN THEORETICAL DIFFICULTY

The role of ideas in human affairs is always subject to varying, and sometimes contradictory, interpretations. Whether nationalism as an idea is a cause or a consequence of social, economic and political changes cannot be definitively settled. At one end of the spectrum, there are those who suggest that, in the overall pattern of events, political ideas have little influence compared with economic, social and technological transformations. Indeed ideas can be largely interpreted as a consequence of them. At the other end of the spectrum, there are those who consider that ideas shape our perception of the world and are the basis of all human action. The approach of this book lies between these two positions by suggesting that people adapt to historical change by inventing or making use of ideas to turn them to their advantage. In this process, some ideas are shown to be more true than others in that they can enable us to understand better the times in which we live and the historical processes in which we are participants.

PLAN OF THE BOOK

Seven chapters are centred on themes rather than a chronological history of the impact of nationalism since the Second World War. Much more can be said on these themes and some guide to the voluminous literature relevant to them is given at the end of the book

The first chapter is on the relationship of nationalism to the Cold War and addresses the question – was nationalism suppressed by the Cold War? The conflict seemed to be one between the 'West', representing liberal values, against the 'East', representing the emancipation of man through socialism. Beneath these banners, were states using nationalism to promote their ends?

The second chapter concerns the reemergence in the 1960s of demands by stateless nations in Europe, sometimes called 'ethno-nationalism'. These have persisted until the end of the century, and achieved some successes. Minority nationalism seems related to a weakening hold of states over the cultural and social values of their citizens. To what extent did this relate to developments in the international system?

The third chapter is about the possible sources of decline of nationalism – European integration and globalisation. In its early stages, Alan Milward has interpreted European integration as 'a rescue of the nation-state'.[8] but, in the long term, the European Union and globalisation may lead to a fatal weakening of the link between state and nation.

The fourth chapter concerns the debates on immigration since the 1970s. Different kinds of nationalism inform the debate, particularly the division between those who consider that a 'nation-state' should be inclusive and 'multicultural' and those who hold that the 'integration' of immigrants is essential, involving their acceptance of the customs, mores and historical memories of the host society.

The fifth chapter poses the controversial question about whether nationalism was a major factor in the break-up of the Soviet Union, the collapse of Soviet hegemony in Eastern Europe and the death of Yugoslavia. Why did nationalism have such wide appeal in the aftermath of these events? Is nationalism an essential element in the modernisation of these societies?

The sixth chapter assesses the impact of nationalism on territorial organisation in the forms of irredentism and separatism. Have these kinds of territorial claim run their course, no longer representing major threats to European stability?

The seventh chapter asks perhaps the most intractable question of all – what role does nationalism have in supporting representative and responsible government? Is the nineteenth-century argument that free institutions are next to impossible in multinational states relevant at the beginning of the twenty-first century? Are systematic appeals to national sentiment a recognition that nationalism is an essential element of democratic politics?

1   The Cold War and nationalism

The Cold War is conventionally regarded as commencing with Churchill's 1946 Fulton speech in which he coined the phrase 'the Cold War' and finishing with Gorbachev's appointment in 1985 as General Secretary of the Communist Party of the Soviet Union. The 'war' was not of uniform intensity or bellicosity and three, somewhat arbitrarily defined, phases are commonly identified.

First, an intense, Stalinist phase (1946–53) in which military confrontation between the West and Soviet Communism was possible and to many seemed imminent. Second, a phase of peaceful coexistence and détente which emerged after Stalin's death with Khruschev's speech to the twentieth congress of the Communist Party in 1956 condemning the crimes of Stalin and the difficult but peaceful resolution of the Cuban missile crisis in 1962. This phase culminated in a major strategic arms limitation agreement but merged gradually into the third phase – a revival of the Cold War in the 1970s and 1980s, with the failure to proceed with the ratification of the second strategic arms limitation agreement, the deployment of Soviet SS-20s in Eastern Europe, the stationing of US Pershing II nuclear missiles in Western Europe, Soviet intervention in Afghanistan, and finally the Reagan 'star wars' project for establishing a defensive laser-based shield in space against Russian nuclear attack. This third phase was also characterised by super-power rivalry in the less developed world with direct military intervention by Russia in Afghanistan and wars by proxy in Africa.

These phases were characterised as much by the mood and atmosphere of international relations as by these iconic events. Events were not tidily distributed into the three phases, since the major event of the second phase was the Vietnam war. But, at the rhetorical level, the language was different; in the third phase, Ronald Reagan condemned the Soviet Union as 'the evil empire', a kind of phrase which no American President used in the second phase. No Soviet (or American) slogan emerged in the third phase to express the desire for mutual accommodation such as that of Khruschev in the second phase of 'peaceful coexistence'.

However interpreted, these phases were far from clear-cut and certain ideological themes persisted through the whole period. These themes seemed both to transcend and to marginalise nationalism. The political elites of the USA and the USSR affected to believe that the Cold War was a confrontation of two radically different political and social projects based on incompatible economic systems. There could be no compromise, at the level of ideas, because the two were mutually exclusive even though the other side could be accepted as a fact of life and practical arrangements could be agreed to avoid military confrontations. Famous dissidents such as Nobel prize winners Sakharov and Solzhenitsyn on one side, Bertrand Russell and Sartre on the other, as well as obscure human rights militants in the communist regimes and peace movements in the western countries, bitterly contested this analysis. But they recognised (and condemned) the dominance of Cold War ideas and slogans.

None of the orthodox accounts of the Cold War consider nationalism's importance. These accounts may be grouped under five broad headings:

*   An ideological struggle between totalitarianism and liberalism
*   A struggle between socialist and capitalist forms of economic organisation
*   A traditional form of great power rivalry
*   The need to expand the role of government in the West, to develop new mechanisms to avoid destructive economic competition, to minimise the role of communist parties and to continue the US domestic wartime consensus into the post-war world
*   The expansionary nature of capitalism
*   The determination of the Soviets to hold on to the territorial gains of World War II – military and ideological mobilisation for war was the only way of doing so

The neglect of nationalism is not because the super powers identified it with instability within their respective Cold War blocs. In the competition for influence in the non-aligned or less developed countries, a wholly pragmatic approach was adopted. Nationalism was designated as good or bad depending on whether the nationalists in question were prepared to accept the leadership of one or the other super power.

NATIONALISM AND UNIVERSALISM IN THE COLD WAR

Since Soviet control in central and Eastern Europe, compared with American in Western Europe, was much more direct, interventionist, and based on force, reactions to it were almost inevitable. Soviet domination was seriously challenged in Eastern Europe by the east Berlin disturbances of 1953, the Hungarian uprising of 1956, the Prague spring of 1968 and the Solidarity movement in Poland in the 1980s. A complex mixture of misjudgements in government policy, popular reaction against oppressive police and political surveillance, material shortages and grievances, as well as nationalist sentiments, were involved in these events.

In the West, the most serious challenge after the 1940s to the solidarity of the North Atlantic Treaty Organisation (NATO) and the American-led coalition did not come from the communist parties, who were effectively isolated by the Cold War. But de Gaulle, a creative and idiosyncratic nationalist, and certain 'neutralists' took a view of French interests that did not always coincide with those of America. The left-wing neutralists and, to a degree, de Gaulle, encouraged a cultural anti-Americanism which pre-dated the Second World War and took forms such as opposition to the marketing of Coca Cola and to the domination of American films in France.[9]

National sentiment and nationalism were clearly present in these major challenges to the hegemony of the two dominant powers. The struggle for freedom from perceived foreign domination as well as specific short-term issues fuelled both kinds of revolt. All of these countries had been occupied or dominated by the Nazis with the consequence that the nationalist sentiments against alien rule engendered by this experience were still very much alive in the 1950s and 1960s. Serious efforts were made by the East European satellite regimes to control and even suppress them. In the West, nationalist ideology was discredited in favour of the rhetoric (and reality) of collective security, international cooperation and European integration. But nationalist sensibilities were expressed whenever a country was involved in armed conflict, such as France in Algeria (1954–62), Britain and France in Suez (1956), and Britain in the Falkland Islands (1982). Moreover, the phenomenon that Michael Billig has called banal nationalism, the everyday flagging of national symbols, images and references to the nation, persisted and flourished.[10]

But the dominant ideas and ideologies of the Cold War seemed, in broad terms, to ignore nationalist principles in favour of universalist claims. They relegated the national idea to, at best, a secondary role and even consigned nationalism to the dustbin of history. The basic question is whether the universalist claims of the free world and of international communism were incompatible with nationalism or were a vehicle for expressing Russian and American national ideas. The intellectual origins of the universalist claims go back to the political ideas of Europe and America in the late eighteenth and the nineteenth centuries. On the American side, the inalienable Rights of Man which included the rights to freedom and self-determination contained in the Declaration of Independence of 1776 and the Preamble to the Constitution of 1787 were the basis of the American constitutional and political tradition.

These values, like those of the 1789 Declar ation of the Rights of Man and the Citizen at the beginning of the French Revolution, were couched in universal terms and were, in that context, those which other nations ought to adopt. The liberalism, constitutionalism and rights-based American tradition rested on axioms considered valid throughout the world. They formed the basis of American propaganda and war aims in both World Wars and were a major impetus behind the Universal Declaration of Human Rights adopted in 1948 by the United Nations. The thrust of American anti-Soviet propaganda was that the Cold War was a struggle for freedom and human rights against those who wished to deny them by use of force and manipulation.

In the Russian case, there was an aggressive promotion of another universalism – scientific socialism. In the celebrated words of the Communist Manifesto of 1848 'all hitherto recorded history is the history of class struggle'; the class struggle would not end except through proletarian revolution and the triumph of socialism. The Soviet claim was based on the ideology of Marxism-Leninism which, it was claimed, had universal validity. Capitalist regimes, despite a veneer of constitutional democracy and legal protection of individual rights, were based on exploitation by the holders of capital of the mass of the population. They denied genuine social and economic rights to the workers; and they were inevitably aggressive because of the structural contradictions of capitalism and because they were bound to try to destroy genuinely socialist regimes. A proletarian revolution would complete the process started by the bourgeois French Revolution and install a peaceful, conflict-free, socialist society. The Soviets therefore claimed to be the camp of peace and the defenders of true human emancipation and liberty.

The Second World War produced a situation in which American liberalism and Soviet communism became the internationally dominant forms of discourse, which influenced all the major actors in the international system. The entry of first the Soviet Union and then the United States into the Second World War had the effect of changing the content of propaganda in the war of ideas to defeat Nazi Germany. Churchillian rhetoric in the early phase of the war, when Britain stood alone against the axis powers, was essentially defensive – a struggle to defend a way of life, an empire, particular institutions and political independence against aggression and against a general threat of barbarism. This rhetoric was broadened to defend the interests of the occupied countries of Europe against oppression and to promote the cause of democracy, in order to sustain resistance to the Nazis in occupied Europe.

Also he particularly emphasised the cause of freedom and democracy to appeal to American public opinion and to draw the United States into the War. This rhetoric was important to show to the British Commonwealth countries that they were fighting not merely to defend the 'mother country' but to promote a common cause. There is little doubt that Churchill and other members of the British elite considered that they were fighting against nationalism and a particularly odious form of it.

THE COMPONENTS OF SUPER-POWER NATIONALISM

Only a minority of Americans would identify themselves as nationalists; like the English, a majority regard themselves as patriots and regard foreigners as nationalists, in any clash with US interests. One recent author, Zelinsky, has, however, persuasively argued that given the 'extraordinary nature of its inception' America can show more of the 'essential nature of nationalism than any other example'.[11] American nationalism (in the sense being used in this book) was forged in throwing off colonial rule and drawing up of a constitution based on general principles. It was consolidated by a civil war (1861–65), preventing the secession of the southern states, fostered by an extraordinary territorial expansion across the American continent (characterised as the 'manifest destiny' of the United States). Economic growth in the nineteenth century and an immense influx of people from Ireland and eastern and southern Europe who, far from being nostalgic for the old country, wanted fervently to become Americans consecrated the establishment of the United States as a great power.

This history has resulted in an exceptional self-confidence, the creation of a strong set of national sentiments among American citizens and adherence to national symbols by most Americans, even though some now see a fragmentation and undermining of this national solidarity by the assault from multiculturalism. The 'American way' became generally regarded as superior to that of other nations. The American federal government funded an Americanisation campaign in the 1920s characterised by a poster campaign in the inter-war period based on the slogan 'There's no way like the American way'; in this campaign, white Anglo-Saxon Protestants were represented as the best representatives of the American way. The 1997 Commission on Immigration Reform recommended that a renewed Americanisation campaign be initiated for immigrants, which triggered both negative and positive responses reflecting two strands in American nationalism.

These two strands both embody attitudes of superiority towards the rest of the world. Both have historical roots going back to the birth of the

Republic, but have acquired particular importance in the twentieth century. Since the rejection by the US Senate of the League of Nations in 1920, the omnipresent isolationist strand of American nationalism becomes dominant from time to time. Isolationism is the view that American should, as far as possible, avoid involvement in matters outside the western hemisphere on the grounds that such involvement is against American interests, will lead to pointless expenditure, the loss of American lives and the possible contamination of Americans by 'un-American' ideas and philosophies. Isolationism is often associated with what Richard Hofstadter called 'the paranoid style in American politics',[12] that is to say the belief that foreign influences should be excluded from American life and that foreigners are constantly plotting to undermine the American way. This way of thinking, although often represented by the hyphenated Americans (Irish-, Polish-Americans, etc.), denounced by Presidents Theodore Roosevelt and Woodrow Wilson at the beginning of the twentieth century in favour of 'hundred per cent Americans', is often associated with an ethnic nationalism. This represents the American nation as derived from north European, particularly British stock, and the further removed from these roots, the less assilimable are immigrants. Legislation restricting immigration since the Chinese Exclusion Act of 1882 has been strongly influenced by this tradition.

The second strand is that it is America's destiny to be the first among nations, to show by example the superiority of the American way, and to assume a world leadership. This form of conventional wisdom held that free institutions, free enterprise, individualism, tolerance of diversity (often now called multiculturalism), separation of the churches and the state whilst adhering to Christian religious values, were the explanation of the rise of the greatest power and the most successful society ever known. The world therefore owes America respect and should follow American leadership. This situation is a burden for the United States because it involves the expenditure of energies, lives and money. Even adopted by successive American Presidents, it has often been difficult to mobilise a majority behind this view because large numbers of Americans have little interest in, or knowledge of, international affairs and indeed in matters outside their own state and locality.

In the post-1945 period, Senator Joseph McCarthy and President Kennedy can be regarded as emblematic figures of these two strands of American nationalism. The former led a notorious witch-hunt against communists and fellow travellers during the first period of the Cold War; he wielded great influence as chairman of two Senate sub-committees, which he used in his obsessive hunting down of communists and fellow travellers in American government and the media. His campaign was halted only when he accused the US Army, itself a powerful national symbol, of harbouring communists.

By contrast, President Kennedy undertook, in his inaugural presidential address, to oppose any aggression by foreign (by implication communist) powers. He said that the United States would not permit the 'undoing' of human rights and, in a famous passage, that the nation would 'pay any price, bear any burden, meet any hardship, support any friend, oppose any foe' to ensure the survival of liberty. This way of thinking led to the beginning of the disastrous commitment in 1964 of American troops in Vietnam.

The dialectic between the isolationists and the 'globalists' is seen in the Congressional conflicts over international organisations, aid and solidarity; it also roughly coincides with the split between those who favour and those who oppose big government and heavy federal expenditure. The League of Nations and the United Nations were set up largely on American initiative but the weakness of the League of Nations was the direct result of American subsequent refusal to participate in it. The refusal of a hostile Congress, influenced by isolationist assumptions, to pay the dues owed by the United States to the United Nations in the 1980s and 1990s has undermined the organisation. The reduction, in the case of sub-Saharan Africa to almost zero, of US foreign and military aid, except in the cases of Israel and Egypt, has contributed to instability in the world's poorest countries.

The burden of the world role was borne more willingly during the Cold War when the Soviet Union was perceived as a direct military threat, and increased arms expenditure under Reagan (1980–8) was tolerated when Marxist insurrection threatened in Guatemala and Nicaragua (traditionally 'America's backyard'). There was also a marked tendency in Reagan to view the world as a struggle between good and evil: the former was represented by all that is best in America; the latter by secret conspiratorial meetings planning world domination, terrorism, drugs, alien contamination and massive influx of Latin immigrants.[13] The obsessive search for an enemy since the end of the Cold War is partly a result of the necessity of finding a threat, credible to broad sections of the American public, to sustain a willingness to pay for supporting a world role. When such a threat is not present, there is marked reluctance to support the use of US troops abroad, as shown by the precipitate 1993 withdrawal from Somalia after the death of eighteen US soldiers shocked American opinion.

Both the isolationist and global role tendencies contain within them strong pressures towards requiring conformity on the part of American citizens. These pressures are normal features of the politics of nationalism. The unique mission of America is supported by a simple, banal, beliefs in the virtues of saluting the flag, 'hailing the chief' (the President and Commander-in-Chief), and in the self-evident superiority of American values. Presidents who took the responsibility for a global role during the Cold War, from Truman through Kennedy to Reagan, unquestionably regarded America as the leader of the 'free world'. This rhetoric has continued, in a modified form, after the end of the Cold War with President Bush referring, on being elected, to America as 'the world's greatest nation' and President Clinton to 'the greatest nation in human history'. This continuing hymn to the glory and universal mission of America is designed to reinforce already existing beliefs and mobilise support for military action overseas such as the (very limited) interventions under both Bush, in the Middle East, and Clinton, in Kosovo. The rhetoric of sacrifice and valour in the service of the nation is necessary to underpin the global role of the USA.

The Russian trajectory has contrasted, in most respects, with the American. The expansion of Russia, from the modest beginnings of the late medieval Duchy of Muscovy, was greater than the American expansion. At its greatest extent in the nineteenth century, it stretched halfway round the world. But it was an empire built by war and conquest, and governed by autocratic tsars. Representative democracy did not take root in Russia until the 1990s and its future remains uncertain. The cement, which held the Russian people together before 1917, was not a democratic project but an autocratic administration and the Russian Orthodox Church. The tsarist autocracy was destroyed by the Bolshevik Revolution of 1917, and the Soviet Communist Party perse-cuted orthodoxy, but both have had a lasting effect on Russian nationalism.

The Orthodox Church cultivated and propagated the belief in the superiority of Russian spiritual values. This belief encouraged the view that Russia should stand apart from the rest of Europe and, with the idea of Moscow as the 'Third Rome', that it was the home of values which were both universal and true. The tsars helped to embed beliefs that Russia was destined to be a great power and yet was vulnerable because it was socially and, above all, technologically backward. The most celebrated of all the Russian tsars, Peter the Great, is an emblematic figure in that he established Russia as a Baltic and European power but, at the same time, was concerned to introduce Western ideas and technologies into Russia. From his reign (1682–1725) there has been a tension between 'westernisers' and 'slavo-philes' which persists today. For westernisers, the salvation of Russia lay in adopting Western ideas and methods in order to become a great power. For slavophiles, the West had to be rejected because it would corrupt what was best and most virtuous in Russia.[14]

The Bolshevik Revolution, however, marked an apparently sharp discon-tinuity in the development of the Russian sense of nationhood. The official communist ideology, as noted above, was both a rejection of the Russian past and a claim to represent certain new universal truths. But there is a parallel, drawn by Leo Trotsky and others, between the French Revolution and the Russian Revolution. Both commenced with an appeal to universal truths but were soon transformed into projects to advance the interests of their respective states and ruling groups. The French revolutionary armies in the 1790s saw themselves not as conquerors but as liberators in the service of the universal principles, Liberty, Equality, Fraternity, and the Rights of Man. They were on a crusade to rescue oppressed peoples from oppression, religious bigotry and aristocratic privilege. In the case of the Soviet Union, the internationalist rhetoric was as strong as with the French revolutionaries, but this time in the cause of the working class, which would overturn capitalism and install a conflict-free, property-less socialist society. This creed accorded well with a certain messianic strand in Russian religious thinking which had contributed much to the sense of Russian nationhood.

Tsarist Russia and the USSR were, however, multinational states dominated by ethnic Russians. After the revolution, the treatment of the non-Russian peoples was justified in Marxist terms but the policy was nonetheless an expression of Russian nationalism. Self-determination for the subject peoples of Tsarist Russia, proclaimed by Lenin in 1917, was quickly abandoned. Priority was given to a defence of the revolutionary homeland against intervention by the Western powers and against the internal threat of the White Russian armies. Russian nationalism (expressions of superiority over other peoples of the USSR and nationalist objectives in foreign policy) reappeared. With the victory of the Red armies over the White armies, securing and spreading socialism by armed force to the old territories of the Russian Empire became the prime objective. The failure of attempts at revolution in West Europe led to the Stalinist programme of 'socialism in one country'. Accompanied by the setting up of the third international of communist parties (the Comintern), internationalist ideology became an instrument of Soviet foreign policy. Russians dominated the Communist Party and the state institutions of the USSR, and the international communist movement.

The official ideology of the USSR also allowed a temporarily successful synthesis between two strands of Russian nationalism, the westernising and the slavophile. The Bolsheviks had adopted from the West both a philosophy and industrial technologies but the Soviet Russian way was presented as at the vanguard of progress and on the path to the future salvation of mankind. As external threats grew more menacing in the 1930s, openly nationalist themes became more evident. Internally, a symbolic change occurred with the dissolution in 1937 of the committee charged with latinising the Russian alphabet. At the same time, the Russian language was designated as the 'international language of socialist culture' together with the adoption of the patriotic teaching of Russian history in schools.

Stalin, having decided that it was prudent to come to an arrangement with Hitler in the Nazi–Soviet Pact of 1939, was surprised by the German attack in 1941 and ill-prepared for it. He had the difficult task of rallying a people, some of whom regarded the Nazis as liberators, to a desperate defence of the Soviet Union. He notoriously changed official propaganda from the building of socialism to the patriotism of 'eternal' Russia. The themes of revolutionary Marxism were downgraded in favour of the defence of the homeland and with this strategy went the abandonment of religious persecution and the mobilisation of religious sentiment in the cause of the defence of Holy Russia.

The superiority of the Soviet system, particularly its capacity to produce tanks, aeroplanes and subsequently missiles, was also constantly vaunted. It was claimed that Russian economic organisation was more just and equitable in that workers were not exploited by private capitalists. These two later became the major themes of Soviet propaganda at the end of the war (and were fervently believed by many Western intellectuals, communists and fellow travellers). They formed the basis of the legitimation of Soviet rule in Eastern Europe in the post-war period. Russian nationalism, the state nationalism of the USSR and the rhetoric of international communism became indissolubly linked in a powerful and threatening combination. There was little doubt in the vast majority of Western political elites believed that communism was an instrument in Soviet foreign policy to promote the domination of Russians over other peoples.

RUSSIAN AND AMERICAN NATIONALISM COMPARED

Russian and American convictions that their nation has unique virtues which should be propagated to the rest of the world have parallels. During the high tide of nationalism, from 1880 to 1914, many German, French and British intellectuals, as well as broad sections of public opinion thought similarly. This conviction disappeared in Germany, at least for a time, with the catastrophe of the Second World War but lingered in France and in Britain, especially in terms of belief in the benefits to other countries of the export of their institutional practices. French universalist rhetoric derived from the Revolution, fully displayed in the bicentenary celebrations of the French Revolution in 1989, and pride in the French cultural tradition made belief in the universal benefits of French civilisation seem more enduring than the British. The British believed in the superiority of their institutions which, they thought, embodied certain political virtues – moderation, tolerance, fair play, integrity, acceptance of the rules of the game. Such a belief contributed to the view that if British virtues and British practices spread to the rest of the world, it would be in everybody's interest.

As already noted, the British (now perhaps only the English) were of the opinion that the British were patriotic whilst other peoples were nationalistic.

This is to regard nationalism as a sort of political pathology, or at least an undesirable political outlook, which provokes tensions and conflicts. This outlook was undoubtedly shared by the Americans and the Russians, who scarcely recognised their own nationalist assumptions, during the Cold War period. The Russians described their struggle during World War II as 'the Great Patriotic War' which inevitably seemed to them a defensive struggle against a virulently nationalist and aggressive power. In the aftermath of the war, they felt menaced by hostile capitalist powers, which possessed superior weapons technologies. Hence they engaged in propaganda campaigns, assisted by Western communist parties, in favour of peace and disarmament. However, they engaged in apparently aggressive acts such as the Berlin Blockade, backed communist-led wars in Korea and Indo-China and ruthlessly suppressed dissent in the East European satellite states. Governments in Western Europe therefore considered that the USSR was pursuing a policy of national aggrandisement under the cover of an internationalist ideology.

The Russians took a similar view of the United States. The rhetoric of the free world, human rights and collective security which was the ordinary currency of American discourse about international relations was usually regarded by the Russians as a blatantly hypocritical cover for American imperialism. The other countries in the American sphere of influence were regarded as being governed by cliques, either dupes or with an interest in the maintenance of the capitalist order. American support for democracy was regarded as a sham because of the American willingness to support dictatorial regimes in Latin America, Asia and Africa as long as they were anti-communist. The Americans gave this view credence by their willingness to collude in the overturning of regimes, whether elected or not, if they were at risk of take-over by left-wing and potentially pro-Soviet groups.

The effect of super-power hegemony on other countries in the two blocs was to turn nationalism into a diet mainly for domestic consumption. The system of blocs suppressed neither the sovereign nation-state nor nationalism but they more or less successfully subordinated them to a wider purpose. Throughout the Cold War politicians and the newspaper press as well as television journalism never ceased to address their audience as members of a nation. This was as true in the Eastern bloc as in the Western. Overt nationalism was encouraged in certain restricted and non-disruptive domains such as sporting competition. The dominance of the hegemonic powers within the blocs was never successfully challenged, except perhaps by de Gaulle in 1966 leaving the military structures, although not the alliance, of NATO. The main difficulties the super powers had with nationalism during the Cold War was in the non-aligned world. Third-World nationalists tended to play one super power off against the other to increase the supply of aid and armaments.

CONCLUSION

The outcome of the Cold War was, in the rhetoric of American presidents and in some academic writings such as those of Jeanne Kirkpatrick, a vindication of America. What happened, according to this school of thought, was an American victory of a particularly comprehensive kind – political, military, moral, foreign policy and economic. This assumption of no particular American responsibility for aggressive actions, except where legitimated by the actions of the other, no major errors in conducting the 'war', and a wholly benign outcome, is the epitome of nationalist discourse. This 'vindicationist' school of thought is not unique and limited to America – it characterised much of the governmental response and early accounts in the United Kingdom to the events of the Second World War.

Super-power confrontation during the Cold War also shows that universalist ideologies are not incompatible with promoting their national interest, sustaining national identity and espousing forms of nationalist ideology. The French revolutionaries of 1789–94, whose role in creating modern nationalism is central, had already shown this to be possible. The compatibility of nationalism and universalism has also been demonstrated in other contexts. The dominance in a population of a universalist religion – Catholicism, Orthodoxy or Islam – has not been a barrier to the success of nationalism and nationalist politicians in a wide variety of countries. A particular country can be represented as the vanguard or the purest form of the religion (France as the 'eldest daughter of the Church', Iran as representing the purest form of Islam, etc.).

One difficulty in understanding of American and Russian nationalism is that they do not conform to any model of the nation-state based on West European experience. The United States is the modern world's first 'new nation' in the sense that it is built on immigration. Others have followed – Canada, Australia, New Zealand – and all have been concerned with the integration of new arrivals and have also been self-conscious about their identity. They have been extraordinarily successful in creating stable political systems, which owed much to favourable material circumstances but also to the cultural process of creating founding myths, images and symbols. This continuing process is best illustrated in the way in which the foundation of their states is commemorated.[15]

Unlike the Americans and the Australians, the Russians did not decimate and marginalise the peoples who stood in their way during their great eastward expansion from the seventeenth to the nineteenth century. But they had an exalted vision of their country and people as 'Holy Russia' which crystallised around three poles – the imperial court, the bureaucracy and the peasant community. The idea of Russia was the bringing together of an unusual combination of elements in a quasi-mystical union. The communist experience transformed these elements but, in a denatured form, they can still be identified in contemporary Russia. Russia and America both demonstrate that the content of nationalisms can take very different, and almost diametrically opposed, forms and that these forms change over time.

2 Nationalism and minorities

The subject of this chapter is national or ethnic minorities, attached to a more or less clearly defined territory. There are, of course, different kinds of minorities. First, there are minorities, such as the Basques or the Corsicans, with homeland which has been theirs for many generations. Second are the groups confined to ghettos because of the attitudes of the majority population, such as the Jews of Eastern and Central Europe before the Holocaust, or because they are immigrant populations, usually poorer than the host population, such as North Africans in contemporary France. Third are the minorities with no territorial identity but which retain strong communications networks such as Gypsies (or Rom people, as they are properly called). The last two kinds are ignored in this chapter, although their treatment by the majority is often an indicator of the virulence of the majority nationalist sentiment found in a country.

The very existence of minorities conflicts with the ideal of a culturally homogeneous national community – for Franco, those who spoke Catalan and Basque were an affront, and a threat to the unity of the Spanish state. This does not mean that minorities have always been subjected to discrimination by nationalists. Small minorities, according to nationalist view, can be well treated as guests, and territorial minorities may be valued provided that they confine the expression of their identities to folklore, music and dance. Liberal nationalists may regard minorities as a fact of life, respecting their identities as part of a liberal belief in universal human rights. Nationalists do not necessarily insist on cultural homogeneity although they generally aspire to one public culture. The cultural peculiarities of minority groups should, in this view, be subordinated to the dominant national culture.

THE ECLIPSE OF MINORITY NATIONALISM AFTER 1945

Small national groups, or fragments of larger nations on the territory of other states, came to be regarded in the 1930s and 1940s, particularly in the countries which emerged victorious from the Second World War, as politically troublesome and as threats to peace and stability. Defeat in war, nationalist revolts and the liberal principle of self-determination had destroyed the multinational empires, which dominated Central and Eastern Europe prior to the First World War. But founding a stable international order on the basis of the national principle was extremely difficult and the inter-war period was troubled by what were called irredentist claims (discussed further in Chapter 6), based on the desire to unite all people of a particular nationality in one state. From the theatrical seizure by the Italian poet and adventurer, d'Annuzio, of Fiume in 1919 to the German invasion of Poland in September 1939, these claims had the potential to plunge Europe into a general war.

The main irredentist problems, such as the Germans in Poland and Czechoslovakia, the Italians of the Dalmatian coast, the Hungarians in virtually all neighbouring states, and the Greeks in Anatolia were resolved, for at least half a century, by the Second World War, the massive expulsions of populations which followed it, and the domination of Europe for four decades by the super powers. However, for two decades after 1945, minorities in Europe were nonetheless portrayed in terms which associated them with treachery, mischief-making, reactionary politics, obsolescent social forms and bloody disputes over territory. This discredit was due to several factors. Small national groups had played a prominent role in the events triggering the outbreak of both World Wars – the assassination in 1914 of the Habsburg Archduke Franz Ferdinand at Sarajevo by a Serb nationalist had precipitated the First, and the inexorable slide into war in 1939 was precipitated by the Sudeten Germans who triggered the break-up of Czechoslovakia, and the Munich capitulation by Britain and France. A disproportionately high number of the leaders of national minority movements threw in their lot with the Nazis in various forms of collaborationist activity in Brittany, Flanders, Alsace, Croatia and elsewhere, in the hope of breaking up existing states and gaining satisfaction to their demands for autonomy or independence. Even though many other minority nationalists resisted Nazi oppression, minorities became tarnished with a reputation for violence and subversion.[16]

This bleak reputation was also partly due to the forgetfulness of the larger nations of their own turbulent and violent origins. In the post World War II period, representatives of larger nations often claimed to have transcended national self-assertion and nationalism in favour of some higher purpose – such as the collective interests of the 'free world', discussed in Chapter 1, European reconciliation and integration, support for international organisations and collective security. The nationalism of minorities was, in this climate of opinion, a regrettable vestige of the past. Most scholarly writing confirmed this view and tended to regard the 'minorities question' as one which was disappearing or would disappear in due course. Louis Wirth, writing in the closing stage of the Second World War, admirably summed up this view.[17] He considered that economic prosperity, the progress of science, the trend towards secularism, and more enlightened social policies were among the factors which would lead to a removal of the disabilities of minority groups and efface their distinctiveness. Modernisation was, according to this view, condemning small national groups to extinction.

Subsequent literature on national and international integration assumed the strengthening of larger political units and, implicitly, the dwindling importance of minorities. In the early literature on European integration, for example, they were completely ignored. In Eastern Europe, where national minorities were potentially destabilising, political aspirations of minorities were delegitimised by the rhetoric of Soviet Communism; those who expressed them were regarded as 'petit bourgeois' and counter-revolutionary and subject to exclusion from the Party and to spells in labour camps. In market economies, economic rationality – the reduction of costs by economies of scale, access to large markets and removal of barriers to profitable capital investment – also seemed to support the cause of large states (and international organisations). Small states seemed condemned either to disappear or become satellites of larger entities. In this climate, aspirations to establish small autonomous or sovereign states seemed retrograde or unrealistic.

The dominant rhetoric of the Cold War discounted political cleavages based on ethnic, linguistic and cultural difference; only those based on ideology or economic interest were regarded as having validity. The politics of the Cold War, emphasising solidarity against a dangerous enemy, delegitimised minority claims as subversive of the common good. The propaganda of both sides occasionally claimed (sometimes with justification) oppression of minorities on the part of the other and supporting minorities was occasionally used as a tactic to subvert the interests of the enemy. The cause of Slovene minorities in Italy and Austria was promoted by the Yugoslav communists to embarrass their neighbours when this was useful to their interests. The Macedonian question was used by the USSR and its most faithful ally, Bulgaria, to discomfort Tito's Yugoslavia. But most minorities were regarded as a marginal phenomenon in the period of postwar reconstruction and into the 1960s.

THE 1960s REVIVAL OF MINORITY NATIONALISMS

Predictions that minorities were doomed to disappear proved incorrect. There was a modest renaissance of minorities and a reassertion of minority claims in Western Europe in the 1960s and 1970s. The disintegration of the Soviet hegemony in Eastern Europe in the late 1980s gave a further impetus to minority claims both in Eastern, and indirectly in Western Europe, the consequences of which have not yet been fully worked out. In the first wave of the 1960s, Basques, Catalans, French speakers of the Swiss Jura, Corsicans, Slovenes of Carinthia, Catholics in Northern Ireland and German speakers of the Alto Adige posed difficult problems for central governments and threats of varying intensity to the existing constitutional order. The radicalism associated with the events of 1968 conferred on minority movements, and the speaking of local languages (estimated as over fifty in sixteen countries of Western Europe)[18] a progressive aura and provided for them a new basis of legitimacy. Although the renewed agitation frequently had the support of only a minority of the minority, it was troublesome because it was difficult for the central governments to assess the causes, importance and significance of these movements.

When minorities speak a different language from that of the majority population, bitter conflicts can arise over language use which envenom other contentious issues. The minority languages of Europe are of two kinds. The first kind is when the minority is spoken by citizens of one state but it is the official, and majority, language of another state. This is the case for French, German and Dutch speakers in Belgium, French speakers in Switzerland and Italy, German speakers in Denmark and Italy, Hungarian speakers in Slovakia, Romania and Serbia, Russian speakers in the Ukraine and the Baltic states and so on. The second kind of linguistic minority is where a distinctive language is spoken and only scattered pockets of the language are found, if they are found at all, outside the regional homeland. Examples are Basque, Welsh, Rhaeto-Romansch (an official language in Switzerland, spoken by tiny minorities in Italy and Austria), Catalan, Langue d'Oc, Irish and Scots Gaelic, and Frisian. Highly politicised disputes have arisen over the classification of minority languages – whether or not they are dialects or *patois*, whether they are independent languages or variants of another language and so forth. Political passions have invaded the scholarly study of languages and language use.

Linguistic homogeneity was an ideal sought by most nineteenth-century nationalists. It was promoted variously in different countries by deliberate government policy or by the spread, through social pressure, of nationalist ideas in the educational establishment. Nationalist attempts to promote a language and discriminate against a minority had spectacular success in France in the nineteenth century[19] and Italy after unification. But the death or the survival of languages is very difficult to predict and language policies do not always have the effects intended. Official support, backed by resources, for a minority language such as Irish and Scots Gaelic may not arrest a long-term decline.[20] Persecution of a language may make the population concerned more tenacious in their determination to preserve the language – Fascist oppression of the German speakers of the South Tyrol and the forbidding of Basque and Catalan under Franco also had this effect.

Factors other than explicit government policies may affect language shift. Government policies, other than those directed at influencing linguistic practice, may produce more rapid or more profound changes. Universal military service, by mixing up populations, sometimes had dramatic effects. The conscripts from Brittany during the First World War arrived in their units speaking Breton and returned after the war speaking French – Breton never recovered. There are economic pressures on minority language use – people may be obliged to speak a language because it gives them access to jobs or because they habitually are selling products in a market where people use a language which is not theirs. If a population becomes convinced that its linguistic practices are marks of social and cultural inferiority, young people may abandon these practices to gain access to a supposedly superior society and culture.

THE ORIGINS OF MINORITY NATIONALISM

Language difference, taken as a distinct factor, does not explain the political aspirations of minorities to self-rule since people speaking different languages can live side by side without conflict, and in some minority political movements language has played little or no part. The effervescence of minorities in the last four decades clearly had some general causes as well as unique and local ones. Minorities were, in part, a by-product of the state building in the nineteenth and early twentieth centuries. This process had the effect of creating minority groups within the large states because homogenisation of the populations of the nation-states was never complete. Economic circumstances, political factors, religious differences and geographical remoteness preserved some minority groups. A sense of being marginalised and disdained explains why some minority nationalists acquired a hatred of the dominant nationality, and this hatred generated violence.

For those in the Jacobin, centralising tradition, based on the principles of the French Revolution, small nations were counter-revolutionary, fostered reactionary sentiments and harboured superstition. Marx and Engels developed this line of thought, considering that small nations were doomed, and that the large nation-state was a stage (characterised as bourgeois rule) on the way to international socialism. Nationalists, whether they were explicitly social Darwinist or not, frequently considered that competition between nations was inevitable and the smaller and weaker nations would not survive. Imperialists believed, in one form or another, that there was a hierarchy of peoples and certain peoples had the predestined role of dominating the others. There was a tendency amongst liberals to regard the defence of small nationalities as reactionary, although certain smaller nationalities in the nineteenth century, such as the Polish, the Irish, and the Orthodox nations rebelling against Ottoman rule, attracted widespread liberal support.

In the more homogeneous nation-states of the Atlantic seaboard of Europe, small nations were, at best, treated with a kind of 'repressive tolerance', to use the term of Herbert Marcuse, and relegated to the position of folkloric or regional groups. The Scots, for example, were submerged in a larger British nation and a spurious prestige was accorded to certain ersatz expressions of Scottishness, such as the kilt and highland dancing. At the other extreme, there was an attempt to extirpate their languages and histories, particularly by using the educational system to achieve this result. In east central Europe there were attempts to ignore them altogether, to treat them as unimportant, as 'peoples without a history'. Thus the Hungarians called the homeland of the Slovaks Upper Hungary and engaged on a policy of Magyarisation, with the effect of stimulating Slovak nationalism.

The turbulence of smaller nationalities in European politics in the second half of the twentieth century has its origin in nineteenth-century political conflicts. Nationalists of small nationalities, as with large nationalities, frequently regard their nation and national struggle as originating in time immemorial. This is true in the sense that peoples with the same names have existed for many centuries and it is possible to find expressions of national sentiments and national antagonisms well before any ideology of nationalism existed. Scottish nationalists see an expression of their political outlook in the 1321 Declaration of Arbroath whose signatories recited the antiquity of their national origins and their resolve to defend their freedom against the aggression of the English kings. The Irish identify the permanent establishment of an Anglo-Norman presence in Ireland in 1291 as the beginning of a long struggle by the Irish people against English rule. Basques believe in a continuous history of the Basque nation, despite virtually nothing being known about it, going back to pre-history, and pre-dating the arrival of Indo-European-speaking peoples in Europe. Most of the East European nationalists under Tsarist, Habsburg and Ottoman rule invented long national histories with scant relationship to historical fact.

This appeal to history and the invention of historical myths played a major role in the creation and diffusion of national sentiment in both large and small European nations. But national sentiment, as presently understood, among the small nations was forged in resistance to alien rule, and underpinned by economic change, in the nineteenth century. The same processes were at work – rejection of the society of estates in favour of the constitution of a nation of equal members – as in the large nationalities. But the smaller nationalities also rejected a dominant nationality, a *Herrenvolk*, which monopolised the key positions of political and economic power. A cultural division of labour was apparent in many places – access to lucrative or profitable activities was made difficult or impossible for members of national or linguistic minorities. By the end of the nineteenth century a sub-elite had emerged among the smaller nationalities who were not prepared to submit to the elites of the larger nations.

For the most part, the large nationalities triumphed as a result of their greater economic, military and political power and the smaller nationalities were absorbed, sometimes assimilated, in states dominated by the large nations. In Eastern Europe, national emancipation in the peace settlements of 1919 was limited by the desire to establish viable states. Some small nationalities, such as the Baltic states of Latvia, Lithuania and Estonia (all absorbed by the USSR in 1940), achieved independence but others were integrated or amalgamated into larger states with some attempt to preserve the rights of minorities. Czechoslovakia contained three national groups (Czechs, Slovaks and Ruthenes) and two national minorities (Sudeten Germans and Hungarians) as well as an important Jewish community. The southern Slavs were amalgamated into the Kingdom of the Serbs, Croats and Slovenes, which also contained Hungarian, Italian and Albanian minorities.

Ireland was an exceptional case in Western Europe, in that an armed revolt and electoral success resulted in secession from a stable and strong state. The British government paid the price, by losing control of twenty-six of the thirty-two counties after the First World War, of both long delay over granting home rule and the error of executing the leaders of the nationalist rebellion of Easter 1916. Attempts by other small nations, such as the Bretons, in the west of Europe to gain a hearing at the 1919 peace conference were contemptuously dismissed. Some of the participants in the peace conferences, in particular Britain and France, were major colonial powers. Already the stirrings of the colonial peoples against imperial domination (some never reconciled themselves to the status of colonised peoples) were apparent in India, North Africa and elsewhere. The imperial powers were firmly opposed to any general right of national self-determination. This position became increasingly difficult to maintain and the colonial empires all disappeared in the thirty years after the end of the Second World War. The emancipation of the colonial peoples, based explicitly on the principle of self-determination, gave an impetus to the movement of minority peoples in Europe. There seemed no reason to refuse to European peoples what was granted to the former colonial peoples, particularly when the decolonisation process was extended to very small populations.

VIOLENCE AND REFORM

Certain West European minorities commenced violent campaigns in the 1950s but electorally important parties regarded them as anomalous relics of past conflicts. The German speakers of South Tyrol assigned to Italy were the first – a violent campaign began near Bolsano in 1956. The Irish Republican Army ran an unsuccessful bombing campaign between 1958 and 1962. ETA – 'Basque Homeland and Liberty' – was established in 1959 and went on to conduct one of the most spectacular and the longest campaigns of political violence witnessed in Europe. Others followed – even in Switzerland, reputed for its peaceful and democratic political system, the francophone minority of the canton of Bern was partitioned to allow the setting up in 1979 of a new canton of Jura, following a campaign which included violent demonstrations and acts of arson. Few European countries were exempt from some form of minority agitation, except countries without territorial minorities such as mainland Portugal and the Federal Republic of Germany (which has a tiny, and highly privileged, Danish minority in Schleswig-Holstein).

The agitation of minority nationalisms was slow to produce results and, indeed, the results have often fallen far short of the more radical claims made on behalf of the minorities. During the 1970s, certain developments held out much promise for the minorities. The death of Franco in 1975 and the democratic transition in Spain led to the reestablishment of the autonomy for Catalunya and the Basque Country which had been lost in 1936. In the context of a general regional reform, Andalusia and Galicia, two other regions with markedly different cultural characteristics, along with Catalunya and the Basque Country, were given special status which they have used to good effect since. Italy followed a similar path, and built on the provision for special regions in the 1947 Constitution, which provided the possibility of greater autonomy for peripheral regions with specific cultural characteristics. The South Tyrol conflict was resolved by a complex package of measures in 1969. This was followed by more regional reforms in the 1970s with staged transfer of power, of budgetary resources and of civil servants to the regions.

In Scotland, the electoral surge of the Scottish National Party in 1967 and 1968 resulted in the setting up of a Royal Commission for constitutional reform and a proposal for substantial devolution. The Left in France became, after a century of adherence to Jacobin centralism, committed in 1973 to substantial regional reform. This eventually resulted in the setting up of elected Regional Councils and an autonomy statute for Corsica in 1982. Developments at the European level encouraged the regional level of government with the setting up of the European Fund for Regional Development and local and regional governments set up pressure groups and consultative machinery at the European level. Finally at the global level two 1976 United Nations (UN) Covenants (one on civic and political rights, the other on economic and social rights) both confirmed the right of self-determination defined not only as a right to sovereign independence but 'the free association or the integration within an existing State or the introduction of another political status freely chosen by the people'.

This burst of activity and optimism was accompanied, and followed, by disappointments and setbacks for the minorities. In those places where the minority nationalist movements had a violent, extreme wing, violence often continued after central governments conceded compromise solutions involving increased autonomy for the regions. This was the case in Northern Ireland where the 1973 Sunningdale agreement, granting autonomy, nationalist participation in government, and an Irish dimension, was derailed by hardline unionists. Another quarter of a century of violence ensued. In Corsica, the 1982 autonomy statute did not meet the requirements of the deeply divided nationalist movement, with the result that sporadic violence, culminating in the assassination of the regional Prefect in 1998, continues. In the Basque country, although the constitutional nationalists gained power in the regional government, ETA continued until the 1999 bombing, intimidation, racketeering and assassination despite expressions of widespread revulsion both in the Basque Country and Spain as a whole.

In other places, many of those affected by the deal struck considered them less than satisfactory. The 1969 package agreement for South Tyrol, whilst it satisfied the German speakers, discriminated against Italian fellow citizens. The rights and jobs reserved for German speakers introduced a kind of linguistic apartheid. This regime also conflicted with generally accepted liberal principles of equal rights for all. The dominant South Tyrolese People's Party preferred to see public-sector jobs remain vacant rather than have them filled by Italians, and to restrict economic growth rather than encourage Italian immigration into the province. In the mid-1970s, this situation provoked acts of violence by the Italian minority. In Scotland the devolution movement of the 1970s failed because, although the 1979 referendum in Scotland resulted in a plurality in favour, the qualified majority required by the enabling legislation was not reached. In France, disillusionment with regionalisation was evident for diverse reasons – its significance was limited by the centralising dynamic of the French administration, very few financial resources were available to the regions, and anxieties existed that it could give rise to further opportunities for corrupt practices.

Beliefs in the retrograde and parochial nature of minority nationalist movements also persisted. These were encouraged, in part, because of the bitterness that conflicts over language use could engender in very different contexts such as Wales, Belgium and even in Catalunya. Deep passions are engendered when issues of language use become politicised. In France especially, the promotion of local languages was often thought by women as a covert way of preserving old social habits which kept them in a subordinate position. Political violence in the cause of minority nationalism ceased to seem a radical, revolutionary act as political circumstances changed. This was the case in Spain after the reestablishment of democracy; the violence of ETA came to appear as the expression of a deep intolerance. Giving priority to promoting the cause of a small nation seemed to undervalue the causes which left-wing, progressive opinion internationally held dear – the struggle against poverty, social exclusion and racism, the promotion of a clean environment, sustainable economic development and a genuine equality for women. Despite having initially attracted support on the political left, the minority nationalists experienced a waning of this sympathy. The events in the Balkans and Eastern Europe in the 1990s (see Chapter 5) led to deep disillusionment with the cause of small nations and to what Tom Nairn has called 'demonising nationality'.[21]

Despite political setbacks, the minority nations made certain gains and further progress was slowly made. National election results have been helpful to the minority cause both in the sense of preventing a right-wing backlash, as in the case of the fortuitous holding of the balance of votes by the Catalan Party when the right returned to power in Madrid in 1997, and the almost contemporaneous arrival in office of governments sympathetic to minorities – Jospin in France and Blair in the United Kingdom. The victory of the former allowed France to sign, in 1999, thirty-nine out of the ninety-eight articles of the far-reaching and important European Charter for the Protection of Cultural and Linguistic Minorities (although the Constitutional Council ruled against the Charter as contrary to the constitution). The Blair government introduced legislation for Scottish and Welsh devolution, approved by referenda, and the first Scottish Parliament since 1707 and, arguably, the first Welsh Parliament ever were elected in 1999. Moves towards the ending of violence in both Northern Ireland and the Basque Country in 1998–9 gave some grounds for optimism that minority nationalism would be dissociated from violence.

EXPLANATIONS OF MINORITY NATIONALISM

It is difficult to interpret certain minority national claims as anything other than the legacy of particular political decisions. This is certainly the case of the claims made by the South Tyrolean People's Party which were the direct outcome of the peace settlement of 1919. But certain general factors were in play as these movements became a more general phenomenon in the 1960s. The radicalism of the 1960s, in the form of student revolts and strikes attacking all forms of established authority, encouraged the minorities' movement. The influence took several different forms. The example of the American civil rights movement had an influence on both the substance and the methods of the minority movements. In Northern Ireland, thirty years of 'troubles' were sparked off in 1968 by a violent attack on a civil rights march (a form of protest copied from the USA) from Belfast to Derry (Londonderry). The combination of constitutional politics and direct action was a feature of the civil rights, feminist and ecological movements, which emerged from the radicalism of the 1960s and were also characteristic of the minority movements.

Many of the minority nationalists explicitly adopted the then fashionable Marxist ideology – ETA and its French equivalent Enbata, as early as 1962–3. This ideological shift was partly due to an anxiety that cultural and linguistic minorities were about to disappear and they could only be saved by the violent overthrow of the existing economic and political order. Radicals and left-wing opinion repaid the compliment by supporting the minorities' demand for the chance for people to stay in their region of origin rather than uproot themselves and lose their distinctive cultures. Both radical intellectuals and representatives of minority nations took up the notion of 'internal colonialism', which alleged that the minority nations were in a colonial relationship with the dominant ones; the 'capitalist oligarchy' of the major nations exploited the 'proletarian minority nations'. Although it produced a lively scholarly debate, it was discredited by empirical evidence which showed that there was no consistent relationship between economic factors and minority nationalism.[22]

Perhaps the most significant input of the radical mood was the undermining of the cultural hegemony of the elites identified with the centralised nation-states. There had been continuing popular reservations and, indeed, hostility to the Oxbridge-educated elite which dominated government, the media (excepting the popular press) and the professions in the United Kingdom. Hostility was evident to its counterparts elsewhere, such as the Parisian elite educated in the Grandes Ecoles and the Paris Faculties, and the Castillian elite in Spain which regarded itself as the true embodiment of Spanish culture and political tradition. The radicalism of the 1960s began a process of conferring legitimacy on other forms of speech and cultural values which had previously been marginalised as expressions of provincial or uneducated social groups. Local languages, dialects and minority cultures were revalued and even became accepted as worth protecting by members of the old elite groups. The cultural monopoly of the elites of the dominant nation has, in most cases in Western Europe, been broken.

This new cultural pluralism may be attributed to the declining nationalism associated with the old nation-states. Whether this decline is taking place remains debatable, especially in the case of England. But the emotional and exclusive nationalism, despite celebrated nationalist figures such as Charles de Gaulle and Margaret Thatcher, which characterised even the mature democracies of Britain and France in the first half of the twentieth century was less in evidence in the second half of the century. The way in which minorities are treated was, and remains, an indication of the strength and nature of nationalist sentiment of the dominant people. Aggressive, domineering nationalists will set out to suppress any expression of an identity different from their own in the territory under their control.

The American treatment of the indigenous population down to the twentieth century, the Tsarist policy of Russification in the nineteenth century, the elimination of local languages through the French school system are amongst the many examples of this powerful integrationist drive. In the 1870s the German historian Heinrich Treitschke gave a classic expression to triumphal nationalism when writing about the recently annexed populations of France: 'We Germans who know both Germany and France, know better what is for the good of Alsatians than do those unhappy people themselves ... We desire, even against their will to restore them to themselves.' In contemporary Europe, no major political party in European Union (EU) member state would express such a position although, in the Balkans, Serbian and Croatian nationalists in the last decade of the twentieth century have been as ferocious in acts as the large nineteenth-century states.

A large self-confident nation imbued with nationalist sentiment may simply ignore small national groups or adopt a protective attitude in order better to assimilate them with the minimum of conflict. But all modern nations are the end products of processes of assimilation of culturally diverse groups and sometimes this has been achieved with great success. This is most obvious in case of nations based on immigration like the United States or Australia; it is very clear in the case of the French, which successfully assimilated a range of peripheral peoples who did not speak French in the first half of the nineteenth century. France, for reasons of demographic weakness, became a country which had, in 1930, a higher proportion of foreign-born immigrants than America and immigrants from other European countries (Poles, Italians, Portuguese and Spanish) have successfully been integrated.[23] The main problem of integration has become the assimilation of large communities of non-European immigrants.

However, the presence of large non-European immigrant communities has indirectly assisted the cause of the territorial minorities. In the advanced industrial societies, it became fashionable from the 1970s to defend the virtues of multiculturalism, to promote tolerant attitudes towards the immigrant groups, fragmenting the 'cultural nation' into a number of cultural groups which all had rights to recognition. This movement began in the United States as a way of removing the prejudices which certain groups such as Afro-Americans, native Americans, Hispanics and Asians suffered from majority opinion. It was difficult for some of these groups to be submerged in the melting pot of American society for reasons of physical appearance or tenacious linguistic practices. The idea of multiculturalism was quickly taken up in Britain on behalf of immigrant groups from the Caribbean and the Indian sub-continent, but with some hesitations. There was, for example, considerable hesitation among the political elite to extend to Moslems the well-established system of financial support to confessional schools.

Hostility to cultural pluralism is a more serious problem in France where the idea of multiculturalism was often specifically rejected in favour of a strict assimilation of immigrants into French culture. The wearing by Moslem school girls of the traditional head scarf provoked expulsions on the grounds of an affront to the secular nature of French state education, a national debate and, in 1993, a very carefully crafted compromise ruling by the Council of State, the highest administrative court. However, there is now a widespread acceptance that cultural pluralism is a fact of life, and that immigrant groups make a distinctive contribution to cultural life, particularly in the domain of popular culture. In accordance with this acceptance, many people across the political spectrum (but especially on the Left) consider local languages should be defended and promoted. The Left sponsored measures such as the recognition the Corsicans as a 'people', and the institution of a 'pays Basque' for the coordination of various policies.

Multiculturalism is grounded in an attempt to defend the rights of individuals and groups to achieve self-fulfilment in the way in which they find appropriate. It has the effect of defending the specific characteristics of all groups which lay claim to cultural specificity. Opponents of multiculturalism argue that it encourages groups in a process of integration in the wider society to arrest this process, and regional groups, with scant contemporary claim to a viable cultural identity, to reinvent themselves. Multiculturalism, the argument continues, can help to maintain community conflicts and work against mutual tolerance although it is not intended to promote tolerance. However, the 'communitarisation' of conflicts can lead to a disintegration of societies, as in the case of Northern Ireland or in Bosnia-Herzegovina. The breaking down of large identities into smaller ones does not necessarily work in favour of individual rights and social harmony.

Changes in the international system have also been regarded as crucial in explaining the rise of minority nationalism. The relationship between it and European integration was first suggested in the 1960s. The two were considered connected because, with the increasing openness of markets and the declining threat of conventional military attack, small-scale independent states seem viable in a way they did not earlier in the twentieth century. States were losing their economic sovereignty and, because of changes in weapons technology, could not assure their own defence without systems of collective security. Also, a greater cultural pluralism seemed appropriate in the context of the move towards a united Europe. Some, such as Denis de Rougement, argued in favour of a 'Europe of the Regions' on the grounds that small political entities would provide greater benefits and be less aggressive than large nation-states.

Initiatives at the European level gave political and moral encouragement to regions and minorities. The European Parliament gave support for minority languages; the Council of Europe sponsored the negotiation of a European Charter for Minority Languages (1993). The European Union promoted the regional level of government in the administration of some of its programmes such as the structural programme and Interreg. The setting up by the 1991 Treaty of Maastricht of an 'Assembly of the Regions' integrated the regions into the EU's constitutional framework. More options in territorial organisation seemed feasible. Independent 'Scotland in Europe' came to appear a practical possibility. The Czechs accepted Slovak independence in 1992, whereas in the 1930s it would have seemed to be folly to the vast majority of the population as well as constituting a serious strategic problem in Central Europe. The proliferation and prosperity of small states worldwide has removed the disdain which German nationalists, and many others, in the nineteenth century had for *Kleinstaaterei* (small statism). Indeed, micro-states have enjoyed a golden age of prosperity and security in the last two decades.

CONCLUSION

The explanations for the rise of ethno-nationalism are various because the cases seem to call for different types of explanation. The same explanations do not seem to apply to Scotland, South Tyrol, Catalunya and Kosovo. General explanations are as difficult to identify for minority nationalism as for other forms of nationalism. Minority nationalisms also take many different forms – some are a revolt against modernity and economic change but others, such as the Scots and Catalans, are forward looking and a successful adaptation to new economic and political circumstances. Some are parochial and resistant to external influences whilst others are open to the outside world and are self-consciously part of an international community of small nationalities. Finally, some are civic nationalists who have a political concept of the nation, such as the Scottish nationalists for whom a Scot is anyone resident in Scotland who identifies with the country, whilst others are exclusionary, ethnic, nationalists. In its various forms and in the new context of Europeanisation and globalisation, minority nationalism is likely to have a continuing impact on territorial politics in Europe.

3 European integration and globalisation

One argument, first expressed in academic literature in the 1960s, has become, in the last two decades, the common currency of political debate. In broad terms it is as follows. Two levels of integration, European and global, undermine certain ideas of the nation and national independence. The European nation-states are considered as being under attack 'from above' by forces in international society and 'from below' by regionalism and separatism. The second, it is argued, has been made possible by the first. The nation-state has lost its autonomy in economic decision making, in defence in culture. Nations diminish in cultural importance as a result of the strengthening of a European identity and above all by the emergence of global tastes and products. Thus, the legitimacy of states based on strong national identities is undermined. However, the nature of both globalisation and European integration are matters of vigorous debate, making this argument, at a minimum, unproven.

A BASIC DISPUTE ABOUT EUROPEAN UNION

The movement towards European integration was initially a deliberate attempt to curb and transcend nationalism in Europe. In the course of a complex evolution of what pro-Europeans call 'the construction of Europe', national interests have often supported moves towards integration. But, at some points, national sentiments have acted as a brake and as a complicating factor.

Since the initial period of European integration, a dispute has persisted between those who believe that nationalism is in decline and that the states of Europe are genuinely pooling sovereignty and those who argue that the nation-state in Europe has been rescued by European institutions, and nationalism continues to be a powerful political force. European institutions, according to this latter view, are an advanced form of inter-state cooperation and not a genuine supranationalism. The extent to which European integration has undermined the sovereignty of states is not easy to assess with objectivity. The belief that it is taking place attracts hopes and fears; it is at the core of political debate and is the subject of a large academic literature.

The dispute will probably be resolved in the early decades of the twenty-first century when the implications of decisions taken in the 1990s have been fully worked out. The main decisions are majority voting in the European Council of Ministers on 'Community' matters, the single currency and the European Central Bank, open borders between member states, and increased powers for the European Parliament. Present indications are that it will be resolved in favour of those who believe that European institutions are a genuine higher level of government, although there is a clear hostility to this in several EU countries, often cutting across the traditional Left/ Right division. The argument continues, with many on the nationalist Right determined to prevent further loss of state sovereignty which others see as either a desirable or an inevitable development. Even if a genuine European government were to emerge, it would not necessarily mean that nationalism was dead, or a political irrelevance, because the most political mobilisation might still be confined within the nation-state.

ORIGINS OF EUROPEAN INTEGRATION

In the 1940s, horror and disgust provoked by the excesses of nationalism manifested by the wars of aggression and the atrocities of Nazism and Fascism were genuine and widespread in European countries. Newsreels of the Nazi concentration camps showing the reality of the attempt to exterminate Jews, Gypsies, homosexuals, communists and political opponents seemed the apotheosis of nationalism. Many of the generation who suffered, and resisted, Nazism and Fascism explicitly rejected nationalism. Emerging from the Resistance movements, a call came for a new European order and a reconciliation of the European peoples. Churchill, in his famous Zürich speech of 1946, championed the cause of a united Europe.

Churchill's vague proposal for the setting up of regional institutions was quickly followed by the establishment, at the instigation of the United States, of the Organisation for European Economic Cooperation in 1948 and NATO in 1949. The Council of Europe in 1949 was an initiative of Europeans, inspired by Churchill. But then, there was a parting of the ways. The main political actors – Monnet, Schumann, Adenauer, de Gaspari, Spaak – who initiated the Steel and Coal Community (1951), the European Economic Community and Euratom (1957), were convinced, unlike the British, of the necessity of creating a European level of government with powers over the member states. The 'Fathers of Europe', as they were often called, were motivated, in this acceptance of supranationalism, by the conviction that nationalism and state rivalry in Europe had to be vigorously combated and the pretensions of the sovereign state to monopolise all political power was dangerous for peace. They believed that a new political form would come into being as a result of an integration process which would result, as stated in the preamble to the 1957 Treaty of Rome, in an 'ever closer union' of the European peoples.

Broadly speaking, four strands of thinking emerged, of widely varying political influence. First, there were those who could not reconcile themselves to the division of Europe into two camps and were inclined to blame United States policy for either allowing or (in a more extreme version) causing this to happen. Fierce opposition to German rearmament in the 1950s came from this tendency – communists, fellow travellers, people of various left-wing views, neutralists, pacifists and some right-wing nationalists. Second, there were those who pressed for genuine supranational institutions promoting a real European Union. Even in the case of the founding fathers of the European Communities, notions of 'national interest' were not far from the surface. They all sought legitimacy for the newly established, or reestablished institutions badly damaged by the experience of defeat and occupation during the War.

But national interests differed – for the first Chancellor of the German Federal Republic, Konrad Adenauer, European cooperation was a way, and perhaps the only way, of reestablishing Germany as an equal and respected member of the international community. For France, European cooperation was a way of controlling and restraining any possible German *revanchisme*. Italy wanted mainly to be treated on an equal footing with the other European powers and to participate in north European economic dynamism. The Christian Democratic and Social Democratic leaders of these countries, after the death of the neutralist German socialist leader Kurt Schumacher in 1952, were almost certainly genuine European idealists but they represented 'their' people and were national leaders without a genuine following outside their own countries.

Third, there were those who were in favour of European cooperation provided it did not touch the core of state independence and sovereignty. This view was represented by the major British political parties. Churchill, despite his stirring call for unity, did not associate himself with further moves to European integration after he returned to power in 1951. Indeed there was some vagueness and ambiguity in his thinking about whether Britain was part of Europe or a separate Atlantic and world power. In the 1940s and 1950s, many government ministers and leaders of different parties across Europe, whilst paying homage to, and giving vague support to the idea of,

European union, did not give it priority. In the first decade after 1945, most politicians were necessarily preoccupied with 'bread and butter' issues – and European union was a rhetorical device to be used on appropriate occasions.

Fourth, some believed that the resistance to German domination during the Second World War was primarily a struggle for national independence. Like de Gaulle, they thought that this independence should not be compromised by American hegemony or by a Soviet takeover or by a revival of Germany or by a project for European integration. This attitude was most explicitly expressed in France, although it was undoubtedly shared by large section of the population of other European countries. In the continental European countries, hostility to the proposal for a European Defence Community (EDC), eventually rejected by the French parliament in 1954, was the defining issue of this last tendency. Several motives were clearly evident in the French debate on the EDC but sovereign control of armed forces was more important for nationalists than any other issue.

From the 1950s to the 1980s, the development of European institutions did not seem to compromise state independence. Indeed, the two seemed to be complementary because the regulation of markets provided by the European Community provided a highly effective framework which allowed the states more effectively to deliver welfare and economic benefits to their citizens. These benefits provided an important basis, along with NATO, which provided a security umbrella, for restoring the legitimacy of the states, badly damaged by defeat and by social dislocation during and in the immediate aftermath of the Second World War. The European institutions, despite a rhetoric of 'supranationalism', did not seem to present a serious challenge to state sovereignty in sensitive areas of foreign, defence and domestic policy. The long period of economic growth, which came to an end in 1973 with the first 'oil shock', helped to mask potential conflicts over free trade in industrial goods and the inefficiencies protected by the common agricultural policy.

Above all, there were clear perceptions that national interests were advanced by European integration. Successive French governments were concerned that Germany should never again be in a position to attack or to dominate France. De Gaulle made Franco-German reconciliation the centre‐piece of his foreign policy in order to further these objectives. The Germans conceived European integration in economic and social matters, and membership of NATO in security matters, as the routes to the restoration of Germany in the community of nations and a position of international influence. Italy, with a weak state, unstable governments and a dual economy, saw a presence in the European Communities as a guarantee of stability, a voice in major decisions and the promise of economic well-being. For the smaller nations, the European Communities were a benign environment because, through the rotating Presidency of the Council of Ministers, favourable representation in the European Commission, Court and Parliament, they have enjoyed an international voice which would not otherwise have been available to them. The EC therefore seemed to complete rather than undermine national aspirations. Only Britain was left out of the game in which everyone seemed a winner.

PERCEPTIONS OF NATIONAL INTERESTS

The way in which President de Gaulle dealt with the European institutions was an apparent proof of their subordination to the states and to national interests. When he returned to power in 1958 it was feared that he would not implement the Treaty of Rome setting up the European Economic Community (EEC). He nevertheless did so for two reasons. First, the common market was in the economic interests of France (it would both assist the modernisation of French industry and protect French agriculture). Second, the European Commission was not, in his view, a supranational authority but an instrument for technical cooperation and coordination of policy. He seemed to demonstrate the subordinate role of the EEC when, in 1965, he challenged his integrationist partners in the other European governments, some of his own ministers, and the European Commission over the issue of majority voting in the Council of Ministers.

De Gaulle simply withdrew cooperation with the EEC, provoking a crisis settled by the 1965 'compromise of Luxembourg'. Thereafter, unanimous agreement between the governments of the EEC was required when vital national interests were at stake. After the accession of Greece and the Iberian states in the 1980s, reaching consensus became increasingly difficult. With the entry of the Scandinavian states and Austria, and above all after the enlargement of the EU to the East-Central European countries, it will become almost impossible. This inevitably led to the situation that de Gaulle resisted – qualified majority voting, entrenched by the 1991 Maastricht and the 1997 Amsterdam Treaties.

The apparent complementarity of national interests and European institutions in the early phase of the European Communities led a distinguished historian, Alan Milward, to conclude that European integration 'rescued' the nation-state.[24] The continental European states emerged strengthened both in terms of effectiveness and of the loyalties of their citizens to them. Others, such as Moravcsik, have argued that the states continue to be the decisive actors in the 'widening and deepening' of the European Union.[25] If nationalism is the loyalty of people to a nation-state, then nationalism was revived and secured by European integration.

However, an important breach had been made in the principle of national sovereignty. Authority was given to Europe to promulgate laws which had direct effect in the member states, with rights of appeal to a European jurisdiction. For a long time, some thought that European law could be rejected by the member states in the national interest. But, in practice, no state resisted the judgements of the European Court of Justice for very long and European law grew in scope and importance. The European Commission represented all the member states in international trade negotiations; it proposed measures in economic and social matters which were accepted by the Council of Ministers and the European Court of Justice existed to adjudicate infringements of European law.

Nonetheless, in the 1980s, Mrs Thatcher came close to repeating de Gaulle's achievement by resisting the European Commission, and all the other member states combined, in her long battle to obtain a rebate on the British contribution to the European budget. She achieved her aim on this issue but she then supported the 1985 Single European Act to complete the single market. It required a vast programme of harmonisation of national legislation to remove non-tariff barriers to trade, which included areas such as health and safety, and gave the European Court a greatly expanded field of competence. To all heads of states and government, except Thatcher, it also implied a move towards a single currency.

The question of whether a new stage had been reached in the integration process was made even more pertinent by the negotiation of the 1991 Maastricht Treaty. The treaty contained a timetable for the introduction of the single currency, and provision for a common and security policy, and closer cooperation in the fields of justice and home affairs. These seemed steps too far for the British government which negotiated an 'opt-out' of the single currency, insisted on maintenance of its frontier controls on persons, and jealously guarded its sovereignty in Justice and Home Affairs. The Treaty was accepted, against the wishes of a vocal minority of the Conservative Party. The Danes rejected the Treaty in a referendum and were only persuaded to reverse their decision by the negotiation of new opt-outs from the single currency, defence, European citizenship and Justice and Home Affairs. The French approved the Treaty in a referendum by a majority of less than 1 percent, after President Mitterrand had campaigned strongly in its favour. German public opinion, and the central bank, manifested strong opposition to abandonment of the mark in favour of a common currency. Only Chancellor Kohl's unshakeable conviction of its necessity allowed a smooth launch of the Euro.

Was the reaction to the treaty of Maastricht a nationalist backlash? It was perhaps more correctly characterised, by a term which gained currency in France, as a 'sovereigntist' revolt. In other words, the objections were largely to granting more power to European institutions, usually referred to simply as Brussels, regarded as too remote, too dominated by technocrats, less accountable, and, in general, less democratic than national institutions. The debate in Denmark was largely about the loss of democratic control and accountability – although the fear that small countries might, in future, be marginalised was probably as important in explaining the outcome of the referendum. In Britain, the undermining of the basic principle of the unwritten constitution, the sovereignty of parliament, was at the centre of the debate. In France it concerned sovereignty of the people, compromised by the introduction of majority voting in the Council of Ministers.

CONTINUING NATIONALIST ASSUMPTIONS IN THE EUROPEAN UNION

Behind concerns about sovereignty, there was a nationalist assumption, namely that the proper unit of government was the nation. Maastricht was seen, correctly, as a turning point in which 'Europe' was emerging as a genuine level of government. Government by institutions where foreigners were in a majority was a major step, conflicting with the nationalist assumptions which most Europeans, especially of the older generations, had not seriously questioned. In the Maastricht debate, national interests, as defined by the governments of the day, were much discussed and the constraints of national political situations featured prominently. Maastricht ratification debate was thus confined to passionate arguments within countries rather than developing into a general European-wide debate. Only the leaders still influenced by the shadow of the Second World War, Kohl and Mitterrand, and active pro-European minorities, often dismissed as 'Euro-enthusiasts', tried to break out of this framework and pose the question of 'what is good for Europe'.

Many themes in the debate were not explicitly nationalist but could be read as coded appeals to nationalist sentiment. Examples are the assertion that the political leaders had advanced too far and fast for public opinion. There was the peculiarly British argument that the Heath government had negotiated entry into the EEC in 1973 without candidly explaining to the British people what it implied. Many alleged that the text of the Treaty was over-complicated and incomprehensible to the ordinary citizen. Finally, there was the allegation that some countries needed European integration in order to reform their economic and political systems whereas 'we' did not.

Other arguments were explicitly nationalist, such as that the Treaty provided a framework for German domination, or that the frontiers of a more integrated Europe would become a 'sieve' through which would pour vast numbers of immigrants. Charles Pasqua and Philippe de Villiers, dissident right-wing Gaullists, spoke openly of 'the suicide of France' in accepting the common currency and the extension of EU competences. The British Eurosceptics strongly implied, when they did not explicitly state, that Europeans (meaning continental Europeans) were foreigners who did not have the same standards and ways of thinking as the British. After ratification the Conservative government moved into an even more negative and nationalist mode and, as Hugo Young observed, its discourse never moved beyond 'complaint, lecture and demand'.[26]

The leaders of governments in the EU were shaken by the popular reaction to the Maastricht treaty and modified both their rhetoric and their actions to avoid giving offence to national sentiment. The Treaty of Amsterdam, which entered into force in 1999 and which was supposed to be a major step forward in reform of European institutions, was a modest affair compared to Maastricht. It gave some increased powers to the European Parliament but above all it sought to give security to those concerned about the spread of criminality and clandestine immigration. The new social democratic leaders elected in the late 1990s adopted a prudent approach to Europe. Tony Blair, perhaps the only British prime minister, excepting Heath, to empathise with Europe, was always careful to say that the British national interest was the sole criterion by which to judge matters such as British entry into the single currency. The French prime minister Lionel Jospin is celebrated for his phrase that he wished 'to build Europe without dismantling France'. Gerhard Schröder, the German Chancellor, adopted a Thatcherite stance towards the German contribution to the EU budget. These, and many other, signs indicated that politicians favourable to European integration nonetheless felt that national sentiment had to be taken into account.

A sense of European solidarity and identity has not yet been established which can rival national sentiment despite the policies designed to bring the EU closer to the people. European symbols have been invented such as a flag, an anthem, a European patrimony of historic towns and sites, and a Europe Day. But a strong European sentiment exists only amongst minorities of public opinion. Majorities in the European Union member countries, with the occasional exception of Britain, Sweden and Austria, are in favour of the Union, but these majorities vary according to economic circumstances. Over the EU as a whole, self-identification with Europe is not strong – 42 percent of respondents to a recent poll said that they identified themselves by their country alone and roughly the same percentage said that they thought of themselves as belonging to their country first and then as Europeans.[27]

Very small minorities identified themselves first as Europeans. In Britain 62 percent identified with their country alone, and 28 percent with Britain and then Europe. Ten countries showed a simple majority of people identifying with their country alone. Five countries – Netherlands, France, Spain,

Italy and Luxembourg – showed a majority identifying first with their own country and then with Europe. Although large populations identify themselves as European there is no evidence that the strong affective bond, expressed in its most basic form by a willingness to fight and die for the country, is yet rivalled by a sense of European solidarity. There is not yet a European *demos* or people.

DECLINE IN THE INTENSITY OF NATIONALISM IN THE EU?

In the second half of the twentieth century, nationalism within the EU member states has lost much of its aggressive edge, although exceptions exist in the rhetoric of Le Pen in France and Haider in Austria. The reactions of the British press and public to the 1999 refusal of the French to raise the ban on British beef, after the EU had declared it safe for human consumption, was aggressively nationalist. However, in general, nationalist passions reach their paroxysm in, and around, the football stadium rather than in politics or on the battlefield. Although national rivalries in Europe remain, they are much less pronounced than they were when the process of European integration began in the 1950s.

The reasons may have little to do with European institutions but lie elsewhere, for example, in the decline of inequalities between states in terms of measures such as gross domestic product (GDP) per capita and a much greater sense of military security. In the 1930s, inequalities of economic resources were striking and brought immediate danger because economic power was immediately translated into military power. Crucially, no EU member now feels militarily threatened by any other member state because war between them has become unthinkable. In terms of economic rivalries, one major European power, Britain, continued a long relative decline from being the richest European country at the beginning of the century to being, at the end of the century, the third or fourth poorest in the EU. This may account for a prickly nationalist resentment, expressed in negative criticism, hostility and rejection of 'Brussels'.

Within the EU, several factors may contribute to the eventual emergence of a sense of belonging to a 'European people'. A new impetus was given to a common external security policy given by the Anglo-French Saint Malo declaration of 1998 and the 1999 integration of West European Union into the EU. The development of an 'area of peace, security and justice' (to use the words of the Amsterdam Treaty) within the EU, and the perception of a dangerous world outside it could contribute to a sentiments of 'European patriotism'. The growing significance of the EU external frontier (except for the UK) for control of movement of persons, and increased police and criminal justice cooperation between the member states, can lead to a sense of a European 'security community', supplanting the security previous provided by the state. A sense of having a clear frontier between 'us' and 'them' is a crucially important factor in the construction of an identity. A threatening external environment has frequently contributed to a strengthening of national solidarity, and this could promote a sense of European solidarity.

The growing impact of the EU on the everyday lives of citizens of the Union through the introduction of the common currency and EU legislation in the economic and social domains may also lead to greater solidarity between peoples. In addition, a great deal of business concerning Europe is becoming routinised – elections to the European parliament, well-publicised European 'summits' (meetings of heads of state and prime ministers). Conflicts which are dramatically reported as 'rows' over policy and important cases before the European Court of Justice bring Europe to the notice of both elite and popular opinion. It is increasingly difficult to imagine a world without the European Union.

A pessimistic scenario for the European Union, in which nationalism revives, is also possible. First, certain economists predict that the economies of the members of the European Monetary Union will diverge. Some may experience rapid growth whilst others move into recession. This is also true of large federal systems like the USA, where some states may be prospering whilst others suffer a sharp slowing of economic activity. However, the much greater mobility of labour within America than within the multinational EU helps to alleviate these differences. In the circumstances of the EU, a single rate of interest can cause grave tensions between states and nationalist sentiment could be mobilised by aggrieved politicians and economic interests. Nationalist reactions are also possible, as a result of differences over policy concerning external trade, particularly if the world's major trading blocs become more protectionist.

Second, the different geopolitical situations of member states could result in divergent approaches to international crises. This has already become apparent when Britain, alone of the European states, actively supported the US air strikes against Iraq in 1998–9 and Greek public opinion, alone of the European nations, overwhelmingly supported the Serbs in the 1999 Kosovo crisis. The enlargement of the EU to include five east Central European states and, possibly, Cyprus will increase the likelihood of these divergences because the West European countries are unlikely to have the same perspective as Poland to a serious crisis in Eastern Europe. This difference in geopolitical situation could also have consequences for low intensity crises, such as the sudden influx of refugees into a particular member state.

Third, the more that the European Union approximates to a state the more it may experience the problems of multinational states in the past. With the abolition of economic frontiers and the fading of political frontiers, socio-cultural frontiers may increase in importance. Proximity of peoples and frequency of daily contacts may increase irritations based on cultural difference and different habitual ways of doing things. Relations between the nations may be stereotyped, simplified and represented by unscrupulous politicians as consistently competitive. National symbols may be defended with greater tenacity if politicians and sections of the population become convinced that they are under attack. An idealised national past may be contrasted with an allegedly detestable process of European 'mongrelisation'.

GLOBALISATION AND CULTURE

The alleged threat of a merging of national identities in Europe has been paralleled by nationalist anxieties about the cultural effects of globalisation – the undermining of national cultures and their replacement by a superficial, rootless cosmopolitanism. According to this argument, a homogenised popular and, indeed, high culture is dominating the rich countries and those parts of the world whose inhabitants can afford to consume internationally available cultural products. The same television programmes are watched all over the world whether via satellite, cable or 'terrestial' broadcasting. American programme makers are by far the most successful and American soap operas, films and popular music are distributed globally.

The super-rich throughout the world bid for the same works of art in the same great auction houses. The most successful living artists cater for the international market place and live notoriously cosmopolitan lives. Nationally based artistic traditions are thus undermined. This tendency is encouraged by the major museums and art galleries of the world, as well as the monuments and historic towns and cities, because they have become international tourist attractions, divorced from the context in which they were created. Tastes are moulded by this internationalisation of cultural life into a similar pattern in all the great cities of the world. High culture becomes a consumer good very similar to other consumer goods. At the level of mass culture, ways of dressing and eating are losing their specifically national characteristics in favour of the ubiquitous jeans, trainers and Macdonalds. The production of similar tastes in consumer goods – clothing, fast food, cameras, television, computers, cars, holidays – is leading to a deliberate search for a 'world style' which will sell anywhere. It is no longer possible to identify a person's nationality by their dress and personal possessions.

An international language – an impoverished form of English – is dominating advertising and communications; all those who wish to participate in the new international society have to have a working knowledge of it. Cultural frontiers between countries, still very clearly defined fifty years ago, have become increasingly permeable and the differences between nations have lost or are losing their sharp-edged quality. The attachment to national histories, cultures, art forms and even languages, which have been important in promoting national consciousness, may weaken. Whether national cultures can survive the internationalising pressures to which they are exposed is a question which is now taken seriously in certain countries, particularly in France where the government demands that cultural products are excluded from all free trade agreements.

There are, however, counter arguments. Whilst it may be the case that there is a strong tendency towards global television, either through direct satellite broadcasting or through viewing the same programmes on many national broadcasting systems, the material broadcast is largely American and is immediately recognised as such. American programmes are interpreted through the prism of national cultural assumptions. The impact of American television programmes in, for example, Algeria, France and Japan, may be very different. In addition, more people may be made more aware, through these programmes, of the cultural differences between themselves and Americans. Some of the research done on such matters as audience reception of the American series Dallas gives support to this view. The image of America communicated through CNN and American popular TV series may actually promote anti-Americanism and nationalism.

THE ECONOMIC AND TECHNOLOGICAL BASIS OF GLOBALISATION

Great technical and economic changes have occurred in the second half of the twentieth century which seem to have accelerated in the last two decades. The technological changes are the radical improvements in transportation, communications and information technologies. Large jet aircraft, satellite television, the development of information technologies – cheap and powerful personal computers, and the world wide web – have affected social organisation and social behaviour across the world. The dissemination of huge amounts of information across international frontiers makes virtually impossible attempts by governments to control information flows.

The general economic changes have deep historical roots such as the expansion of international trade and the international division of labour, based on comparative advantage, which resulted in an interdependence of economies in the nineteenth century. Among the changes in the late twentieth century are the growth in the importance of international or multinational companies, the integration of financial markets, the freedom of capital flows, delocalisation of production of major manufacturers either to sites close to major markets or to countries with cheaper costs, the influence and global presence of major consultancy firms, such as Arthur Anderson and Price Waterhouse, and the impact on national decision making of world institutions such as the International Monetary Fund (IMF), the World Bank and the World Trade Organisation (WTO).

The exponents of the globalisation thesis frequently argue as though the globalisation of the world economy is a self-evident truth. But there are counter-arguments. One such argument is that multinational companies are multinational in appearance only. There are American, British, German or French companies with international operations but which have a solid and secure base in the countries in which they have their head offices. In terms of capital flows, critics of the globalisation thesis argue that the nineteenth century had an equally free global capital investment, greatly assisted by the gold standard which was the basis of international unit of exchange. Even the greatest capital exporters, Japan and the United States, have not yet reached the proportion of the GNP exported from the United Kingdom at the beginning of the twentieth century. The critics of the globalisation thesis also argue that there have always been relationships of economic domination and dependence, with the economically powerful subordinating the weak; the new international economic institutions merely disguise the balance of economic strength and have not seriously affected traditional relationships. The apparently global economy is, in reality, an American-led system.

The increase in world trade has not led to a more genuinely integrated world market in either manufactures or in agricultural products. Efficient agricultural producers encounter protectionist regimes in Japan, where until recently the import of rice was forbidden, and in Europe, through the Common Agricultural Policy. Most of the increase in world trade has taken the form of an increase in the trade of manufactured goods – often very similar sorts of goods such as motor vehicles – between the advanced industrial countries. The rest of the world – particularly the poor countries of 'the South' – are left out of this expansion. The critics of globalisation will usually concede that there has been a change in the pattern of foreign direct investment in that manufacturing units have been set up in other countries to take advantage of cheaper costs and the proximity of markets. But, it is argued, this only affects certain sectors, such as automobiles, and is a more marginal phenomenon in terms of total manufacturing output than is generally realised.

Critics of globalisation also argue that, although governments' freedom in making economic policy is restricted by the markets, and a debt crisis results in highly visible intervention by the International Monetary Fund, the constraints on governments have not grown as much as is argued. As with cultural globalisation, the reality of economic globalisation is contested but there is little doubt that governments feel increasingly constrained by market forces and by trade agreements through the World Trade Organisation. If the nation-state loses effective control over all major economic policies this will have profound effects on national identities.

A TENTATIVE CONCLUSION

The relationship between European integration and globalisation is not clear and a variety of political positions on it are commonly expressed. Both processes are of great concern to nationalists. Extreme nationalists, such as Le Pen in France, are against both, but some British Eurosceptics regard globalisation positively because they see it as providing a means of escape from a European 'superstate'. Other nationalists regard the EU as a defence against the potential ravages of globalisation and against the domination of the United States.

A dynamic of European integration is now well established and this makes the further progress of European integration look almost inevitable. But whether this happens depends very much on 'events', particularly in the broader, global context. Global crises – economic, financial, military, demo-graphic, environmental – could either strengthen the European level of government against the nation-states or it could tear the European Union apart. Whether the nations of Europe are more or less immutable features of the European polity, or whether a European identity can or will emerge which will replace or co-exist with the various national identities of Europe, are questions which can only be answered by future developments.

Despite European integration and the alleged importance of globalisation, the defenders of the nation occupy offices in government in the EU member states. In France, the socialist prime minister, Lionel Jospin (*le Monde* 14 January 1999) said

> The nation is an irreducible reality, the heart which sustains democracy, the space in which a social bond is created and where the strongest solidarities are forged. We must preserve the personality of France ... France cannot live without its own identity ... only the respect for her identity will allow France to enter fully in a future which she wishes to control.

Open opponents of European integration in France, such as Charles Pasqua and Philippe de Villiers, are electorally influential.

Strong anti-European, pro-national sentiment is expressed in Britain. The anti-European theme was tersely expressed by Thatcher in her famous speech in Bruges in 1988 when she rejected any notion 'of suppressing nationhood and concentrating power at the centre of an European conglomerate'. In January 1999 William Hague, in a major speech, tried to re-define Britishness away from the sentimental imagery of John Major, his predecessor, towards a multicultural, creative, enterprising image of Britain. He launched a new Conservative Party programme entitled 'The Battle for Britain' – against any weakening of the Union between the nations of the United Kingdom and against the encroachment of the European Union on British sovereignty. In general, especially in Britain and France, globalisation and European-isation are, in political discourse, more likely to be Aunt Sallies than warm and attractive images.

4 Nationalism and immigration

Immigration is one of the great European debates of the last quarter of the twentieth century. In the period from the end of the Second World War to the 1973 oil shock, there was increasing political tension on the subject in the prosperous countries in northwest Europe – Britain, France, the Netherlands and Germany. In the case of Britain the real debate ended before 1973 with the introduction of severe controls on immigration. But the 1981 Nationality Act, the 1999 Immigration and Asylum bill and the difficult adjustment of the UK to the Schengen agreements allowing free movement between the EU member states, show that major questions have yet to be resolved. By the 1990s, all countries of the European Union were affected by immigration but, within them, the debates took different forms.

Nationalism permeates the debate on immigration because one of its basic tenets is that the nation, however large or small, has clearly defined limits, in terms of both territory and membership. People are divided into those who belong to the nation and those who are excluded from it (aliens may become members of the nation after a formal procedure of naturalisation, usually lengthy, and, in some cases, impossible). Governments and parliaments are sensitive about the role of the European Union in the areas of immigration and citizenship because of a widespread conviction that governments have the right to decide whom they accept both as residents and as citizens. Nationalists therefore have serious reservations about the introduction (five years after the entry into force of the Treaty of Amsterdam) of majority voting in the field of immigration in the European Union.

Nationalist beliefs, in their strong forms, are defended, at least by minorities, in all European countries. The vast majority of the population of these countries share moderate nationalist assumptions because attachment to a nationality and to a state is generally assumed to be necessary both to enjoy rights and to be secure. Vague nationalist sentiments are also important because aliens are less trusted than fellow nationals because either they are not committed to the same values, institutions and interests or because, in some sense, they are foreign. But the various ethnic, legal, territorial and cultural components of nationality have different meanings within and between European countries. In political debate, people take different views about their relative importance and passionate controversies can, and do, develop.

GROUNDS FOR REFUSING IMMIGRANTS

There are two general objections to the acceptance of immigrants – racial and cultural. Although analytically distinct, when expressed as unreasoned prejudices, they are often indistinguishable. The objections to non-white immigrants derive partly from racist beliefs and partly from perceptions of cultural difference. Racist beliefs are based on ancient prejudices, strengthened by nineteenth-century scientific and anthropological doctrines, about the inequality of races. In the early twentieth century, these doctrines were almost universally believed to be descriptions of fact. Aboriginal peoples and Negroid Africans were placed at the bottom of the racial hierarchy, after which came Orientals and Indians, with the white, usually north European races, at the apex of the hierarchy. There was also a tendency to believe that nations were biological groups with different inherited characteristics, genetically distinct from other nations. Racist nationalism accordingly was given a pseudo-scientific basis.

The implication of racism is that members of other human groups cannot be assimilated and become like 'us'. The vast majority of German Jews were only too ready to assimilate and asked to be accepted by the host community. But the Nazis rejected them, despised them and eventually exterminated them because they regarded Jews as incontrovertibly other – a corrupted and inferior kind of human being. The racist, therefore, recognises (in the case of non-white people) or invents (as in the case of the Jews) biological characteristics which prevent assimilation – the alien must therefore be excluded and miscegenation forbidden. Nazi racist policies and the advances in the science of genetics discredited these beliefs but they linger on in popular consciousness. In the late twentieth century, in public, only neo-Nazis and extreme nationalists, such as Jean-Marie le Pen, have been prepared to state openly that they believe in the inequality of races.

The proposition that people of different colour and appearance are culturally different was, in most cases, well-founded until a relatively recent past. The inter-mingling of peoples, the global economy and the global communications industry has made this assumption less true. However, different physical appearance is often an important element of self-identification and identification by others in contemporary Europe. European nationalists will tend to trust non-white people less either because they do not have the same attitudes and loyalties or because, in some other general sense, they are different. Even when they are, for example, British or French citizens, their loyalties are still questioned. A hierarchy of cultures is often assumed to exist and supported by the fact that culturally sanctioned ways of behaving in some non-European societies are not tolerated in European countries. Examples are circumcision of young women and polygamy. This leads to the position that, if others are admitted to our societies, they must abandon some of their habits and customs.

France has been a 'melting pot' in the twentieth century but successful assimilation of immigrants requires acceptance of the dominant values of French society and the norms sanctioned by the French state. Any evidence of non-acceptance creates a widespread reaction against the immigrants concerned. The building of mosques, female circumcision and polygamy, the intrusion of religion into the public domain, all produce high levels of disquiet and sometimes indignation. Government policies of assimilation in all European countries imply that cultural differences must be confined within certain limits. Unlearning old habits and learning new ones is a slow process and, in some cases, progress is measured over decades and over generations. In other cases, this is not so because some immigrants are desperate to shake off the past. As Arthur Miller, the American playwright born of Jewish immigrants, has put it, virtually none of those Jews who left the *shtetls* of Eastern Europe for America had any nostalgia for the old country because life was too hard there; hunger and violence were ever present dangers. America was regarded as infinitely superior. The EU has a similar image for Albanians and Kosovars today.

The practices of states with regard to immigration in post-Second-World-War Europe conform to nationalist assumptions in two important respects. First, a crucial function of frontier controls has been to exclude foreigners who are insufficiently documented (and perhaps suspected of trying to become illegal immigrants), or deemed politically undesirable, or unwelcome because suspected of criminal activities. Second, states, until recently, have exercised the uncontested right to determine who can stay in the country and who can accede to citizenship. In the past, there was no obligation for the state to give reasons for exclusion, although, if immigrants gain access to the territory of the state and then are expelled, all EU member states will now, in theory, give reasons for doing so. Some rights of appeal, if an individual has succeeded in entering a country, exist to contest the accuracy and the legality of the reasons given.

Perceptions of national interests and views about the usefulness of immigrants influence the ways in which states exercise these exclusionary functions. The national interest is usually based on a notion of security –

whether immigrants and applicants for citizenship are a risk to the security of the state and public order, and whether the individuals are likely to engage in activities detrimental to the country. Economic considerations also have a role – are they needed as workers, professionals or business people? Economic interest has been very important in practice, since the flow of immigrants into European countries has been closely linked to the demand for labour, but the debate on immigration has rarely been dominated by economic or cost/benefit considerations.

Shifts in policy in the last fifteen years in Europe have been linked to changing perceptions of these interests. Particularly in the field of security, a shift in the perception of the issues has resulted in immigration coming to be regarded as a common European problem as a result of free movement within the EU. Also, influential figures are now warning that, for demographic reasons, Europe may need more immigrants in future. The perception of immigration as a European problem is, however, far from complete and reactions in the major countries to questions of immigration, without taking account of the EU, still loom large.

BRITAIN, FRANCE AND GERMANY COMPARED

In the quarter of a century after the Second World War, immigration was a pressing issue for countries experiencing the end of colonial empires. Immigrants from colonies or former colonies tended to gravitate towards the 'mother country'. Britain put severe limits on immigration before the economic difficulties of the 1970s because of the end of empire and the expected reaction of the British electorate to the 'problem' of immigration. Whilst the British empire lasted people from the Commonwealth countries, colonies and dependencies were regarded, for most purposes, as subjects of the British Crown and had unrestricted rights of entry and abode with full civic rights in the United Kingdom. Informal measures were nonetheless taken to prevent the immigration of non-white people. This theoretical openness contrasted with the restrictive rules applied to aliens (non-British subjects) introduced by the Aliens Act of 1905 and subsequent amendments to it, which allowed the immigration service to exclude any foreigner without explanation.

But the openness did not survive the end of empire and the growing problem of hostility to the immigration of non-white people from the Caribbean and the Indian sub-continent. West Indians started to arrive in the UK in the late 1940s. London Transport in particular had an active policy of recruiting them. The numbers were relatively small. By 1959, about 126,000 non-white immigrants were estimated to have arrived in the UK. The number of non-white residents in the country then increased quite rapidly because of new arrivals from the Indian sub-continent, family reunions and the fertility of the immigrants who were mainly young adults. There was nonetheless nervousness in official circles about popular reactions to them, even when their numbers were low.

Consideration of how to restrict non-white immigration had started under the post-war Labour government, but the Conservative government's 1962 Commonwealth Immigration Act placed severe restrictions on entry. The Act applied to the old (white) Commonwealth as well as to the new (non-white) Commonwealth countries, but the exclusion of non-whites immigrants was the scarcely disguised objective. This caused an agonised debate between representatives of liberal opinion who thought racism was repellent and foreign to British traditions of tolerance and those who felt restrictions were prudent because of widespread colour prejudice, particularly among the working class. In the 1960s many who were previously liberal on the issue changed their minds. The most prominent was the former Conservative Cabinet Minister, Enoch Powell, who in 1967 spoke of 'a nation building its own funeral pyre' and of 'the river Tiber foaming with much blood' if further immigration, even of dependants of immigrants already in the country, was allowed.

All politicians became alarmed by the possible electoral consequences of immigration. When, in 1967, British passport holders of Asian origin were expelled from East Africa, Parliament passed legislation within a week to withdraw the right of residence in the UK to certain categories of British passport holders. Only British passport holders resident in or with close connections with the UK were to have unrestricted rights of entry to the UK. Subsequent legislation in 1971 and 1981 formalised this. When Hong Kong returned to Chinese sovereignty in 1997, the British designated 100,000 rich or well-qualified Chinese who would be welcome in the UK (very few, in the event, wished to come). This removed the last great source of mass immigration from British overseas dependencies. The British government in 1999 revised its position on the few remaining British passport holders in dependent territories (e.g. Falkland Islands, Gibraltar) and proposed to allow them unrestricted entry to the UK.

The history of British regulation of immigration was one of ad hoc measures, strongly influenced by electoral considerations. Nationality or citizenship (the notion of a British subject, still present in the Nationality Act of 1948, effectively disappeared with the end of empire) was much debated but there were no consistent principles underlying legislation. The sense of the 'Britishness' of the peoples of the empire, even those of the old white dominions, quickly dissipated once the memory of the common struggle against the Germans and Japanese began to wane.

A hard line on immigration control, a refusal to engage in European cooperation on movement of persons and an attitude which characterised anti-racism as 'wet', became prevalent among the Thatcherite Conservatives. Some were inclined to cast doubt on the Britishness of non-white British citizens, as when Norman Tebbit proposed his notorious cricket test – only those who supported England were truly British.[28] The Labour Party, partly as a result of its own record in office and partly because many of the more anti-immigrant voters were amongst its electorate, became extremely cautious on immigration policy. The closing of 'loopholes' against further immigration remained a priority which the Blair government continued, with its 1999 tightening up of the procedures for dealing with asylum seekers and immigrants.

The French situation differed from that of Britain because of a contrasting form of imperial rule and a different concept of citizenship. The French legacy of direct rule of most of its empire, the assimilation, in the 1946 Constitution, of parts of the empire into France by the creation of overseas *départements* (which still exist), all contrasted sharply with the British tradition of indirect imperial rule which respected the different cultural traditions of the subject peoples. The French civilising mission was conceived as giving the colonised peoples the benefits of French education, law and administration. Belief in the universalism of French values contrasted with the localist and specific nature of the British/English tradition. The result (together with French notions of citizenship) was a much more integrationist and assimilationist policy vis-à-vis the populations of the overseas possessions than was the case for Britain.

The main principles underlying French citizenship emerged in the course of the nineteenth century with some modification in the late twentieth. The 1789 Declaration of the Rights of Man and the rhetoric of the French Revolution suggested that the nation was a form of political association which could be joined voluntarily. Indeed, distinguished foreigners, such as Benjamin Franklin and Tom Paine, were granted French citizenship during the Revolution of the late eighteenth century. However, practice differed considerably from the principle of citizenship open to all. During most of the nineteenth century, only those children born of French fathers were considered French until a law of 1889 granted automatic citizenship to children born in France of foreign parents. From that time, French citizenship could be acquired by descent, place of birth and residence. Immigration was welcomed by employers and the French state, because of the country's demographic weakness, although there was some hostility at the popular level – riots against Italian immigrants took place in the 1890s.

After 1945, although the French birth-rate increased sharply, immigrants were still arriving in significant numbers. Immigration was relatively loosely controlled by administrative regulation (although the acquisition of residence and work permits was often a trial for individual immigrants) and a buoyant labour market attracted immigrants from a number of sources in the 1950s and 1960s. However, tensions grew between the French indigenous population and North African immigrants after the Second World War. From the middle of the 1950s, as a result of the independence gained by the protectorates of Tunisia and Morocco and, above all, by Algeria (which was, in principle, part of France), exacerbated these tensions. The failed attempt to integrate Algeria into France, brutalities on both sides during the war (1954–62) and the flight of French settlers at the end of it led to a deep mistrust of Algerians, and of North African Moslems in general, although many Algerians resident in France had acquired French citizenship. Negative attitudes toward North Africans and Moslems have persisted ever since.

The flow of immigrants from Algeria was reduced by agreement with the Algerian government, and by administrative controls. But the number of immigrants coming from the former colonies in sub-Saharan Africa increased. The ghettoisation of both black and Moslem immigrants led to increasing tensions between immigrants and the host population. The imposition of severe restrictions on immigration in 1974 was therefore relatively uncontroversial because of widespread hostility to immigrants and because of a general view that jobs did not exist for them. These controls never wholly succeeded and estimates suggest that the rate of immigration continued to run at the level of 100,000 per year. In addition to the official immigrants, a large number of undocumented immigrants (officially estimated at about 300,000 at the time of the 1998 amnesty) have been present in France.

Anti-immigrant sentiment increased in France in the 1970s and 1980s for a combination of reasons. The economic justification for immigration seemed to disappear. Large sectors of the population regarded non-white and Moslem immigrants as unassimilable. The main reasons were criminal problems, which seemed to be particularly linked to areas with high immigrant populations; terrorist activities by groups from the Moslem countries led to widespread alarm, and consequent repressive action on the part of the governments seemed to stigmatise all immigrants. Violence against non-white immigrants became a common occurrence which anti-racist campaigns, despite their high profile, did not prevent.

This situation was fertile ground for political exploitation by nationalist politicians. The National Front, led by Jean-Marie le Pen, became a significant and threatening political force from the time of the 1986 parliamentary elections. Hostility to immigration and immigrants was the major appeal of the National Front whose electoral campaigns were often accompanied by violence against immigrants. By the middle 1980s, le Pen's party was the equal (in terms of votes) with the Communist Party, and came to represent the alienated and socially insecure. The appeal of a truculent nationalism and hostility towards the politicians in place, coupled with an anti-immigrant platform was, within certain limits, electorally profitable.

This success of the extreme Right caused divisions within the 'respectable' Right. The more nationalist, anti-European politicians wanted to do electoral deals with le Pen or tried to outbid his anti-immigrant policies. Charles Pasqua, on the right of the Gaullist Party until he defected in 1998, was Minister of the Interior in the early 1990s: he proclaimed a policy of 'zero immigration' and introduced measures in 1993 to make it more difficult for children of immigrants to acquire French nationality. As an opposition politician in the late 1990s, he also attempted to divert support from the National Front to the mainstream Right by adopting anti-European themes. Nationalism seemed in the ascendant but it was also deeply divisive since some leading Gaullists and right-wing Republicans were pro-Europe and in favour of more liberal immigration policies. The Left was also divided, with a nationalist anti-European Jean-Pierre Chévènement as Minister of the Interior who also adopted a hard line, when he could, on immigration and on cultural difference. He was supported by communists, and others on the Left, against the majority of socialists who were pro-European and moderately pro-immigrant.

The problems confronted in Germany were very different. The massive expulsion of Germans from the eastern territories in the immediate post-war period provided an adequate supply of labour in the short term immediately after 1945. But, from the 1950s to the 1970s, there were labour shortages as a result of the rapid growth of the German industrial economy. When the supply of Italian immigrants declined sharply with the beginning of the Italian economic 'miracle' at the end of the 1950s, Germany entered into a number of agreements with other Mediterranean countries. The intention was to recruit contract workers, the *Gastarbeiter*, who would return to their native lands after a maximum of two or three contracts. But this did not happen – these workers stayed and were frequently joined by their families and children were born in Germany.

When economic conditions changed in the 1970s, the German government (sensitive to historic memories of Nazi treatment of foreign workers) was reluctant to engage in large-scale expulsions and few of the immigrant workers were willing to go voluntarily. They were tolerated but their situation was not regularised. The possibility of long-term residents becoming citizens was closed to them because the German citizenship law was based on *jus sanguinis*, in other words on a blood connection. Ethnic Germans from Eastern Europe, often not speaking the language and without recent family connections with the country, had automatic right of citizenship under Article 116 of the 1949 Basic Law (the German Constitution). Access to other immigrants and their children were subject to drastic restrictions. These were modified in 1991 and in 1999 German citizenship law recognised *jus soli* – people born in Germany could claim citizenship, and the conditions for permanent residents becoming citizens were liberalised.

This reform came after a very troubled period in relations between some sections of the German population and non-Germans. After the 1989 unification of Germany, Turks, sometimes resident for decades in Germany, Poles, non-white asylum seekers and Gypsies were the targets of increased racism and violence. Given the twentieth-century history of German racism, the violence provoked concern, both in Germany and abroad. The enormous increase in asylum seekers in the early 1990s was regarded as only a partial explanation of the violence against them. The Christian Democrats (CDU and especially the Bavarian CSU) became firmly committed to stemming this flow as well as stopping clandestine immigration. The Social Democrats and the Greens gave priority to a better integration of the immigrants already in Germany. For them, the reform of the nationality law was an essential element of this but they also agreed that tight control of immigration and asylum seekers had become necessary.

Similar themes have been debated in the other European countries, centring on 'bogus' asylum seekers, the influx of refugees fleeing violence and penury, clandestine immigration, and the assimilation of immigrants already on the territory. These debates occurred somewhat later in the southern EU member states – Portugal, Spain, Italy and Greece. The southern states had traditionally exported rather than imported people. The populations of these countries had the reputation of being less prejudiced against non-white people and more generally hospitable to foreigners than their northern neighbours. However, by the 1990s, open hostility towards black Africans was common in Italy. Even in Portugal, where there had been a long practice of miscegenation with colonised peoples, prejudice against immigrants appeared. Strong pressure from their northern partners encouraged them to introduce immigration legislation (Italy, for example, had none until 1990), data protection legislation so that information could be shared on individual migrants, and readmission agreements to accept return of illegal immigrants who had crossed their territory to reach another member state. By the mid 1990s, there was also electoral pressure on these governments to take restrictive measures.

EUROPE AND IMMIGRATION

Developments at the European level are beginning to make inroads into the sovereign control which states previously exercised. The 1957 Treaty of

Rome, containing the famous four freedoms of movement of 'labour, capital, goods and services', implied open access to the labour market of member states by citizens of other member states. In the long term, this meant the abolition of frontier controls on persons between EU member states. This occurred with the 1996 entry into force of the 1985 and 1990 Schengen agreements. Systematic checks on people moving from one EU member state to another, except when they enter the Anglo-Irish free travel area, were abolished. The controls at the external frontier of the Schengen area were strengthened and subject to common rules.

The implications of the Schengen agreements, and their integration in the Amsterdam Treaty, are far-reaching for all countries except the UK and Ireland. All citizens, whether they are economically active or not, can reside in any other member state. States have given the responsibility to the other member states for checking on individuals who enter their territory from non-EU member states. They have agreed to common rules for issuing visas, for asylum (in the Dublin Convention) and have declared that they will move towards a common immigration policy. Once third-country nationals are on the territory of the EU it is difficult to prevent them moving freely between the member states (although they often do not have the legal right to do so). They have set in place improved systems of information exchange, and police and judicial cooperation to deal with problems which may arise from the open borders. States are the executive agency on policy concerning the free movement of people but this policy is decided at the European level – at the moment by unanimous agreement but, in five years' time, by majority vote.

Access to citizenship remains the responsibility of the states. 'Nations' therefore still decide who they will accept as members. But there is now a measure of uniformity in the principles of access to citizenship since the 1999 German nationality law – a mixture of *jus sanguinis*, *jus soli* and natural-isation – although the administrative details may vary. The integration of basic rights into the Amsterdam Treaty may eventually give the European Court the right to review the naturalisation procedures of the member states. At present, the concept of an 'EU citizen' is limited to equality of economic and social rights across the EU, and the right to vote in European and local elections for residents in other member states. Nonetheless, a start has been made to detaching both the notion of, and the law on, citizenship from their strict association to the nation-state.

CONCLUSION

The existence of a common external frontier, an embryonic common immig-ration and asylum policy, free movement within the EU and the idea of a

European citizenship are contrary to core tenets of nationalism. Nationalists have the choice of ignoring, minimising or contesting them. An example of ignoring them was the virtual absence of recognition that the UK was a member of the EU in the 1998 White Paper *Fairer, Faster and Firmer: a Modern Approach to Immigration and Asylum.* The minimisers take the view that the developments are marginal and far-removed from the sentiments and beliefs of ordinary citizens who remain firmly attached to the nation-state. They also take the view that European measures should go no further than the stage they have presently reached. On other occasions nationalists contest the existing free movement provisions vigorously – for example, in the 1993 French Senate debate on the ratification of the 1990 Schengen Convention, the charge was vigorously made that it was a danger for the French nation.

Europeanisation of these policy areas is a genuine break with a nationalist past in which states, acting on behalf of the nation (however defined), had sovereign control over who entered the national territory and on what conditions, and who became a member of the nation and a citizen of the state. The realisation that a radical change is taking place has not yet become part of popular consciousness across the EU member states. Since the arrival of unwanted immigrants attracts great media attention, often out of all proportion to the size of the problems posed, this is potentially dangerous for the EU. The hostility to these immigrants is inspired by nationalist sentiments – 'they have no business being in our country'. The possibility now exists that anti-immigrant feeling will be deflected towards the European Union, thus weakening the popular acceptance of European integration.

5 Nationalism and the break-up of the Soviet Union and Yugoslavia

The collapse of communist regimes in East Europe caused a major reappraisal of nationalism. A demon of extreme and aggressive nationalism, which many in the stable western democracies believed dead, was unleashed. The USSR and Yugoslavia, two internationally powerful multinational states, which previously seemed to be successful in persuading people of different nationalities to live together, fell apart. Czechoslovakia went through a 'velvet divorce' and two sovereign states, the Czech Republic and Slovakia, succeeded it. More ominously, violence between national groups became commonplace in the Balkans and in parts of the former USSR. The twentieth century had commenced with 'an age of nationalism' and was terminating with a resurgence of nationalism, with destabilising consequences.

The events of 1989, which initiated the collapse of communism, and their aftermath came as a surprise, except to a few perceptive Cassandras. As Walter Laqueur writes '... of all the factors which brought about the downfall of the [Soviet] union, nationalism was, by and large, the one to which least attention had been paid.'[29] For seventy years, Soviet nationalities' policy seemed to work and was credited with a large measure of success by non-communists. An immense multinational state was created in which Russians predominated, but in which the languages and cultures of other national groups were protected. If the regime was oppressive, it oppressed all in equal measure. Nationalities thought to be hostile to communism, like the Volga Germans and the Crimean Tartars, were ruthlessly repressed and deported *en masse* by Stalin but a similar fate was visited on Russians who opposed or who offended the regime. There was evidence of a particular form of virulent nationalism – anti-Semitism – at the popular level and in the Communist Party during the Soviet period. The most notorious official expression of prejudice against a national/cultural group was the 1950 doctors' trial when the accused were Jews.

Amongst the general population, anti-Semitism and Russian chauvinism towards other national groups survived, and minority nationalities were under-represented in the Communist Party and the institutions of the Soviet state. If an empire is defined as a multinational grouping in which there is a dominant nationality then the USSR, with a population of about 290 million when it broke up, with just over 50 percent Russians and over 100 other nationalities, qualified as an empire. Minority nationalities tended to identify the ruling institutions as Russian. But the Congresses of the Communist Party and the meetings of the Supreme Soviet were great gatherings which represented the ethnic and national diversity of the USSR. Unlike the multinational empires of the past, the country was apparently an example of a multinational state without unmanageable centrifugal tendencies. Most observers thought that this was also true of Yugoslavia.

The Soviet nationalities' policy consisted of recognising the existence of nationalities, their languages and their cultures, and making the territorial division of the country reflect, as far as possible, the distribution of nationalities. Stalin, as commissar for the nationalities, proclaimed in 1917 the equality and sovereignty of all the peoples of the former Russian empire, the abolition of all religious and racial privileges, the free movement of all nationalities and ethnic groups within the country, and the free development of the national and ethnic minorities. He went as far as to support the right of self-determination. Finland and the Baltic states took Stalin at his word and declared their independence, during a period when the new regime did not have the military force to oppose them. But Stalin and Lenin intended to keep as many of the old possessions of the Tsarist empire, to ensure the security of the new regime. They aimed to create a multinational state as a stage on the path to building an international socialist society.

In the view of Lenin and Stalin, the way to maintain the unity of the USSR was to promote the cultural and economic development of the nations, some of which remained in a pre-capitalist stage of development. Soviet rule brought real economic and social gains to many nationalities – electricity, literacy and the emancipation of women were amongst these – and this helped to build a loyalty to the USSR. Mixed marriages, the promotion of bilingualism (with Russian), the intermingling of nationalities in the cities and industrial areas was thought to promote easier relations between the nationalities. Recruitment to the Communist Party and involvement in party affairs also increased contact between the nationalities. However, Soviet nationalities' policy was widely interpreted in non-communist countries as a cynical alibi for promoting one-party totalitarian rule. The practice of Soviet communism was indeed, in most respects, unrelentingly centralist.

Basing themselves on Marx and Engels, Lenin and Stalin developed a particular view of self-determination. Self-determination should be the expression of the will of the labouring masses and it should assist the promotion of socialism. This interpretation ruled out demands for self-determination of which the Communist Party leadership disapproved. Self-determination, included in the Stalin Constitution of 1936 and the Brezhnev Constitution of 1977, was a right which never had a chance of being exercised. Both constitutions envisaged a federal structure in which the nationalities were recognised. For Stalin, federalism was not an enduring principle of political organisation but a stage on the way to a unified socialist society. In practice, the states of the federation were tightly controlled by a highly centralised Communist Party. The only genuine recognition of the nationalities and ethnic groups was therefore in the cultural and linguistic fields. However, the constitutional right of self-determination, the establishment of a federation with the boundaries drawn roughly along national lines, and the encouragement given to national languages had a role in the final disintegration of the USSR.

For almost seven decades a strong and ruthless central power kept national/ethnic conflicts in check. Strong empires seemed to have done this for a time in places notorious for inter-communal conflict – in Cyprus, between Greeks and Turks, in Palestine between Jews and Arabs, and in India between Moslems and Hindus. When the imperial or central power declined, bloody conflicts followed. The weakening of Communist Party and the Soviet state apparently caused this history to be repeated. Hélène Carrère d'Encausse published in 1978 *l'Empire Éclaté* (the fragmented empire) in which she predicted the end of the Soviet empire because it had failed to reconcile and integrate the different nationalities, in particular, the Moslem nations of central Asia. She interpreted the USSR in a way which highlighted parallels with the European colonial empires which all disappeared in the mid-twentieth century.

At the time she wrote, this view was widely regarded, particularly in left-wing circles, as a piece of wishful thinking or as anti-Soviet propaganda. The subsequent turn of events launched the author into international fame and into the prestigious French Academy (she was only the third woman Academician in 350 years). Her book published in English in 1993, *The End of the Soviet Empire: The Triumph of the Nations*, was concerned to show that persistence of national sentiment had brought about the disintegration of the USSR. Similar interpretations were encapsulated by the title of Ronald Grigor Suny's book *The Revenge of the Past* (1993). The old demon of nationalism, it was argued, appeared once the heavy repressive mechanisms of the Soviet state were removed and the machinery of repression no longer operated with its previous violence and ruthlessness.

This view is plausible because the practice of Soviet rule contributed to maintaining national identity whilst attempting to eliminate all vestiges of what was termed bourgeois nationalism. This was done in four ways, all of which had the perverse effect of encouraging the kind of nationalism which the system set out to extirpate. First, the promotion of bilingualism in practice made knowledge of Russian obligatory, a continuation of the unpopular Tsarist policy of Russification, initiated in the second half of the nineteenth century. Second, the encouragement of publication in the minority languages, intended to fight illiteracy, fostered an awareness of national differences. Third, the nationalities acquired their own universities, academies of sciences and intelligentsia, all with an interest in preserving their influence. Fourth, the nations and ethnic groups were recognised in both the constitution of the USSR and the constitution of its largest component element, the Russian Federal Republic.

Similar assessments were made about the Yugoslavian model of socialism with its decentralisation of power, accompanied by workers' self-management. However, the Yugoslav Federation broke up with dramatic speed after 1989, in national conflicts whose violence seemed a reversion to previous dark periods of Balkan history. Yugoslavia fragmented on national lines and the successor states aspired either to a homogeneous national population or a policy that subordinated other nationalities present on their territory to the dominant nation. Where neither was possible a bitter conflict ensued, as in Bosnia-Herzegovina, or an uneasy peace prevailed, as in Macedonia, or ethnic cleansing took place, as when the Croats expelled the Serbs of Krajina and Western Slavonia. Ethic cleansing by the Serbs provoked external intervention in both Bosnia-Herzegovina and Kosovo.

In reading Yugoslav history backwards, it is very easy to see the process of disintegration as inevitable. Excepting the period of Tito's rule (1945–80), pessimistic statements were frequently made about the viability of the state. Before 'The Kingdom of the Serbs, Croats and Slovenes' was founded in the aftermath of the First World War, Percival Dodge, the American representative to the Serbian government, wrote in 1917 'all those who know the three nations express doubts that they could unite happily in one state'. Tensions, degenerating into acts of violence, between the national groups appeared soon after the founding of the state. Throughout the history of Yugoslavia some Croatian groups worked towards the independence of Croatia, and a Croat client state was briefly established by the Nazis. Croat militias were responsible for massacring Serbs in large numbers during the occupation, a fact which was bitterly recalled by the Serbs in the final crisis of the Yugoslav Federation over forty years later.

Tito, sometimes described as the only real Yugoslav, understood the problem and sought to reduce the predominance of the Serbs by creating a federal republic of six states. He drew the boundaries of Serbia narrowly so that Serb populations were left in the neighbouring states of Croatia, Bosnia Herzegovina and, to a lesser extent, Macedonia and Montenegro. The autonomous regions of Vojvodina and Kosovo were established within Serbia to reduce Serb control of these ethnically mixed areas. As with Stalin's USSR, the federal structure was largely a constitutional fiction in the early years of the state but in the 1960s a genuine federalisation commenced which gave real authority to the governments of the states. The Communist Party itself became federalised to a degree, so that the party leadership in the states was largely composed of members of the dominant nationality. Only the army escaped this process of decentralisation and federalisation.

In both Yugoslavia and the USSR, nationalist agitation was suppressed by an iron hand – the combination of a totalitarian party, a strong state apparatus and a secret police, all imbued with an anti-nationalist ideology. Those who believe nationalism caused the disintegration of these states, consider that authoritarian rule of these societies was bound to weaken in the long run and the nations would inevitably reassert themselves. The disintegration of the two countries gives some support to the simple view that nations are primordial human groups and that repression alone prevented nations from seeking self-government. Many involved in the violent conflicts in both ex-Yugoslavia and the ex-USSR, believed that this was the case. Other participants, who did not approve of the fragmentation of these states, believed there was a pathological nationalism behind the forces of disintegration. One of Yeltsin's staff in 1993, at the constitutional conference, which established the Council of Independent States (CIS), described it as 'a form of political aids'.

In order to answer the question whether the reversion to nation-states was inevitable, a review of other possible explanations is required. The most influential explanation is that of authors – Nairn, Hobsbawn, Benedict Anderson and others – influenced, at least in their youth, by Marxism. These authors do not agree with each other about nationalism, but a general position can be derived from their writings – nations like social classes are constantly being created, disappearing or being modified. Nations are the outcome of political and, above all, socio-economic processes. Often they reinvent Karl Deutsch (1953): when people communicate within a group more easily than with individuals from other groups, then the main condition for the formation of national consciousness is laid. On the basis of a dense communications network, a nation develops a whole range of collective memories, symbols, flags, anthems, songs, traditions (often invented), and collective ambitions.

This view, therefore, sees nations as continuously re-made or re-shaped. Nations did not emerge unchanged by decades of communist rule – on the contrary, they were profoundly modified by the communist experience. There is evidence to support this view. The relations between the nationalities during the communist period in both states evolved as a result of economic and political change. Under Khruschev (1953–64) and culminating with Brezhnev (1964–82), and in the last stages of Tito's rule, much power was ceded to, or was acquired by, the local national elites who ran the constituent republics of the USSR and the Yugoslav Federation. Despite occasional purges of the Communist Party, these elites became increasingly corrupt, and some adopted a lavish lifestyle. Corruption, clientelism and nationalism were closely associated as the party leaderships defended their own power base. The nations were redefined in a struggle for survival, influence and resources.

The centre (the state and party organisations in the capital) and the dominant nationality came to believe that exploitation was by the periphery of the centre. This was the reverse of the stereotypical situation in traditional empires where the centre exploited the periphery (the colonial possessions). The dynamic western Republics of Yugoslavia and the non-Russian southern Republics and Baltic Republics in the USSR seemed to benefit from investment, cheap energy and labour migration. The poorer Republics also seemed to benefit – they acquired 'unjustified' subsidies from the centre. The richer nationalities, such as the western Republics of Yugoslavia, considered that they were being unfairly taxed to support both the bloated central government, and the poorer, undeserving eastern regions. These feelings became bitter and divisive because of the huge disparity of GDP *per capita* which was as high as 7:1 between Slovenia and Macedonia – similar regional disparities were found in the USSR. The rich nationalities looked down on the poor especially as a result of internal migration – the Bosnian (Moslem) shanty towns in Ljubliana (Slovenia) were regarded as evidence of innate fecklessness. All the national groups therefore came to believe, for different reasons, that they were being exploited. This caused the growth of a defensive, and new, nationalism to prevent further exploitation by the supposed beneficiaries of the system.

Another explanation of the collapse of the regimes (especially the USSR) was based on the nature of technological change. This explanation may well have appealed to Karl Marx himself, since he argued that the 'modes of production' (roughly technology plus forms of organisation) determined the organisation of society. Increasing Soviet technological backwardness, impossible to rectify in a command economy, has been suggested as a cause of the disintegration of the system. The centralisation of economic decision making was well adapted to mobilising a backward society to create great primary industries in the Stalin period – coal, steel, oil exploitation, textiles, transportation, electricity and, above all, armaments. It was ill adapted to create industries which responded to consumer demands and incapable of making internationally competitive industrial goods.

The technological backwardness became catastrophic with the 'information revolution' based on computer technology. This could neither be efficiently developed nor effectively used in a command economy. The new technologies resulted in increased complexity, incompatible with the Soviet system because of the immense expansion of information and the need for decentralised decision making. It was relatively easy for the USSR to acquire new computer hardware, despite American bans on export of strategically sensitive material. But exploiting hardware depended on small groups of entrepreneurial software engineers. The application of programmes by technologists, managers, producers and distributors, used to receiving instructions defining their tasks, was simply impossible without a change of both organisation and of mentalities.

Tight political control of the population was made more difficult with relatively simple recent technological innovations such as the photocopier and the fax – the capacity to transfer huge amounts of information by computer links made it impossible. The attempt to adapt Soviet practices, based on Gorbachev's concepts of *glasnost* (transparency of information) and *perestroika* (restructuring), was a response to the new 'modes of production'. But to increase the circulation of information was incompatible with the attempt to retain the Communist Party's monopoly of power. As a result the Communist Party control, and the system as a whole, collapsed. Communist party *apparatchiks* wishing to retain power, and those seeking to replace them, could not find an alternative to mobilising national sentiment. Defence of interests and, in some cases, simple material survival could only be secured by ethnic mobilisation in a society faced, in the 1990s, by catastrophic economic collapse. This 'technological determinist' explanation is compatible with the post-Marxist explanations in that the nations of the USSR and Yugoslavia are being 're-created' by a new set of circumstances.

Other explanations focus on the specific situation of the two countries. In the case of the USSR, Paul Kennedy's thesis of 'imperial over-reach' is pertinent.[30] The Soviet leaders had created an empire and aspired to a global role in competition with the United States. The Soviet Union was a vast territory, stretching across eleven time zones, containing about one-sixth of the world's inhabitable area, and over 100 nationalities. Resources on a massive scale were needed to govern, police and defend this territory. In addition, dominating the East European countries, engaging in an arms race involving ever more expensive weapons, creating a navy to show a Soviet presence in all the world's oceans, building a space programme to demonstrate that the USSR was as technologically advanced as the Americans, subsidising prestige activities such as sport, engaging directly in a war by intervention in Afghanistan, and wars by proxy in Africa and Central America, was to engage in activities which could not be sustained by the Soviet economy. This analysis was the basis of the Reagan administration's policy of 'arms-racing the USSR to the negotiating table', in the belief that the Soviet Union could not afford to do what it was doing and would be forced to negotiate.

A similar, and equally persuasive, explanation can be suggested for the break-up of Yugoslavia. The country emerged from the Second World War with a claim to have liberated itself before the arrival of the Red Army. It was, for a brief period, a loyal member of the Soviet bloc before breaking with Stalin in 1948. Thereafter, Tito's Yugoslavia was constantly under military and ideological pressure from the USSR, which retained a powerful military presence in neighbouring states. To maintain legitimacy for his regime, Tito posed as a leader of the non-aligned nations and devoted considerable diplomatic and political activity to this role. The external threat, the repression of political opponents, and Tito's international standing helped to maintain the unity of a fragmented society. But the situation required an excessively large military and internal security capability, as well as resources to play a global role. The developed western regions, Slovenia and Croatia, became increasingly unwilling to bear the costs involved.

The last explanation is that the whole of the Marxist-Leninist and Titoist projects were doomed from the beginning. The collapse of these systems was an inevitable outcome of their misconceived and false ideological foundations. Before the collapse, this position was widely regarded crude anti-communism. After the collapse, it gained in credibility. Some conservatives had long considered, in the manner of Michael Oakeshott, that Marxism and its variants was an extreme example of 'rationalism in politics'.[31] It could not work, according to this argument, because it was based on a misunderstanding of politics and human nature. The attempt to impose a blueprint on societies was based on the erroneous belief that historical laws had been discovered. Francis Fukuyama proposed a variant of this view – liberal democracy had simply conquered rival ideologies because it was superior, and this victory marked the end of ideology.[32]

Closely related to the position adopted by Fukuyama was the view that the regimes were fundamentally flawed because they had an economic theory which was simply wrong. A well-known figure, the Anglo-Austrian economist Friedrich Von Hayek, had argued this from the 1930s but his views did not become fashionable until the 1980s. Neo-classical economists, influential in the 1980s, considered that the market provided the only form of economic rationality. Attempts to replace the market by a planned economy inevitably lead to gross economic distortions and economic collapse. Most, like Milton Freedman, considered that a regime such as that of the Soviet Union could not adopt a market mechanism without fundamental political reforms. These reforms, in broad terms, should establish a liberal constitution in which the economic role of the state should be confined to regulation to ensure that the market operated efficiently. Such reforms would lead it in the direction of Western liberal institutions and the rule of law, thus abandoning communism.

Whether there was a real alternative to the collapse of the Russian economy and the chaotic political condition of Russia in the 1990s may be questioned. But the argument that economic mismanagement of the world's richest country, in terms of raw materials, led to the collapse of the USSR is a strong one. The Soviet Union lost the economic Cold War and lost it decisively. It could not feed its own population without substantial grain imports from the United States; it could not produce internationally competitive manufactured goods; it did not satisfy basic consumer demands in the country; and it could not keep pace with America in the arms race of the 1970s and 1980s. A similar argument can be made about Yugoslavia whose economy became increasingly uncompetitive from the 1960s and the country became weighed down with massive external debt. The gross internal economic distortions, in both the USSR and in Yugoslavia, could not be addressed within the existing political system.

CONCLUSION

There are a number of plausible general explanations for the collapse of the USSR and Yugoslavia. To future historians, they will all doubtless seem oversimplifications but each contains important insights. Some give little importance to the role of nationalism or national sentiment as a root cause of the collapse of these systems. They regard nationalism as an epiphenomenon and not the basis of an explanation of the transformation of the USSR and eastern Europe. National identity is regarded as malleable and changing over time; national sentiment and nationalism were no more than useful instruments in the circumstances surrounding and following the collapse of communism. Nationalism triumphed because there were no competing ideologies. It also served as a tool for maintaining a minimum of social cohesion. In the explanations sketched above, nationalism assisted these societies to move from closed authoritarian systems in the direction of more open democratic societies.

Yet accompanying the demise of communist regimes, national conflicts of murderous virulence took place. Resentments were engendered about matters which could not apparently be negotiated. 'Ethnic cleansing' entered the vocabulary when peoples in Yugoslavia who had lived peaceably side by side for decades decided that this was no longer possible and set themselves on a course of physically eliminating minorities. Neither the Serbs nor the militants among the Albanophone population of Kosovo considered it worthwhile reaching a political compromise, despite the huge cost of the alternative. Small nations confronted larger ones in a wide variety of situations. Sometimes they were successful, at least temporarily, against all the odds, as when the Chechens made military victory too costly for the Russians in 1996–8. Formerly obscure peoples caused general surprise when they declared independence from fragments of the USSR such as when the Gaguaz (Christians of Turkish origin) announced separation from the newly independent Moldova and elected their own parliament.

It is difficult to dismiss the expressions of nationalism in the former Yugoslavia and the USSR as mass delusions, having little to do with the basic causal factors in play. The actors in these political dramas stand accused of having little or no understanding of the real issues at stake. Marx invented a term for this blindness – 'false consciousness' – and the distinguished interpreter of nationalism, Ernest Gellner, has argued that nationalists rarely have much insight into the roots of nationalism. Gellner's contention may be correct but nationalist passions, and nationalist interpretations of who their enemies are, play a major role in what happens. In this sense nationalism is a factor, and an independent factor, in the evolution of events and is not merely an expression of processes which are unknown or hidden from most of the people involved.

6 Irredentism and separatism

The most important claim that can be made for nationalism is that it changed the political map of Europe in the nineteenth and early twentieth centuries. In the late twentieth century, however, there has been a change – modifications of the frontiers between states has become a rare occurrence. The upheavals in Eastern Europe, following 1989, created new states but without changing frontiers because the successor states respected, in ex-Yugoslavia with much difficulty, the internal boundaries of the states from which they emerged. Seizing territory by armed force, a commonplace until the end of the Second World War, is now very difficult, as the Israelis have discovered. This represents a major change in the international system and has important implications for nationalism.

Nations historically were forged by armed conflict which either brought together disparate territories, as in the United Kingdom and France, and assimilated, with more or less success, the peoples who inhabited them, or, as in the case of Germany and Italy in the mid-nineteenth century, unified culturally similar peoples. Violence seemed inseparable from state and nation building, and the two seemed interconnected. Has this process run its course? Does relative territorial stability mark a weakening of nationalist ideas and passion? Are national identities being shaped in ways other than war and violence? Is it possible that new identities may emerge but as a result of different processes to those of the past?

TERRITORIAL CLAIMS

In the nineteenth century and first half of the twentieth century, the most common territorial claims by nationalists were based on irredentist and separatist demands. The first, derived from the Latin *terra irredenta*, was for 'unredeemed land', territory which belonged to a people by right but was under the control of another state. This claim was based on the assertion that the inhabitants of this territory were culturally and linguistically part of the nation. But it could also mean, as in the Italian case, that the territory was necessary to the well-being, security and even the survival of the nation.

Italy after unification in 1866 claimed that the 'natural' or strategic frontiers of the nation were along the crestline of the Alps – although the territory included a large population of non-Italians, such as the German speakers, who were in a large majority in the South Tyrol. The Irish nationalists, who gained an incomplete independence in 1922, wanted the whole island of Ireland because it was a natural entity, despite the fact that the majority of the northeast of the island clearly wished to remain part of the United Kingdom. The Unionists were, and some of them remain, prepared to engage in violent action to resist being integrated into a nationalist Ireland.

Separatist claims were made by movements seeking to free peoples from alien rule so that they could acquire independent statehood. Greeks, followed by a series of peoples of east central Europe, successfully asserted this right in the nineteenth and in the first two decades of the twentieth century. The process did not provide greater peace and stability. 'Balkanisation', meaning the creation of a number of smaller states by the fragmentation of larger ones, became a term of disparagement because it seemed to produce disorder and insecurity. Balkanisation was disapproved of in the foreign ministries of the major states and was regarded as a real risk for new independent states of Africa. This was why most official international opinion, with the partial exception of the French, was hostile to separatist movements which threatened the Republic of the Congo, in the attempt to create an independent Katanga (1960–3), and the Federation of Nigeria when, in 1967, the separatist standard of revolt was raised in Biafra.

A more general claim, which briefly assumed a sinister reality, was the claim that each nation was entitled to a *Lebensraum*, or living space. This supposedly scientific argument, first advanced by a German geographer, Frederik Ratzel, in a book *Geopolitik* published in 1897, was that every people needed 'sufficient' territory for its survival and to support the specific cultural forms associated with it. He also argued that frontiers were an indication of the relative power of nations and that stronger nations inevitably claimed and won territory from weaker ones. Both claims, as expressed by Ratzel, had much evidence to support them in terms of the behaviour of the European powers in the nineteenth century. His disciples, such as Karl Haushofer, extended these arguments to justify Nazi conquests of territories to the east on grounds of racial superiority as well as the economic and strategic needs of Germany.

Hitler himself adopted the view, very similar to that of Haushofer, that force not persuasion is the fundamental factor of change in human affairs: 'The broad mass of the people – wants the victory of the strong and the annihilation or unconditional surrender of the weak' (*Mein Kampf*, pp. 371–2). German apologists for the Nazis attempted more elaborate justifications for an expansionist policy. A spurious Nazi historical anthropology attempted to show that the Polish lands to the east were originally inhabited by Teutons who had been pushed westwards by barbarian Slavs. Arguments about who were the original inhabitants of a territory have been commonplace in the history of nationalist propaganda. Irish nationalists have argued that the original inhabitants of Ulster were Irish Gaels, and the majority Protestant population of Northern Ireland were colonists. The Greeks have claimed land which was part of classical Greece even though there were no Greeks there. The Zionists claimed Israel although between their expulsion in the second century and the mid-twentieth century there was only a tiny population of Jews in Palestine. In these cases the actual inhabitants of the territories were regarded as latecomers whose claims were illegitimate.

Nazi ambitions to expand to the east were defeated on the battlefield, with the result that between ten and twelve million Germans were expelled from eastern territories which had been settled by Germans for many generations. But German geopolitical ideas, and their adoption by Nazis, Fascists and others, explains why nationalism, which was regarded by many Europeans in the nineteenth century as a enlightened and progressive, came to be thought of as irrational, threatening and destructive. In the words of a distinguished Royal Institute of International Affairs (1939) study of contemporary nationalism, it was a threat to peace and to the very future of civilisation. It also came to be linked with the breakdown of democracy. All the European dictatorships established between 1918 and 1939, with the exception of Béla Kun's short-lived Marxist revolution in Hungary in 1919, espoused some form of nationalist ideology.

During the Second World War, the Nazis aspired to change the map of Europe by annexations such as Alsace from France, dismantling countries such as Poland and Czechoslovakia, directly exploiting the occupied territories and their non-German peoples, and creating client states, with the help of separatist movements, such as those in Croatia and Slovakia. This redrawing of the political map was accompanied by a policy of racial purity which involved killing Jews, Gypsies, homosexuals, the mentally ill and physically disabled. The Nazi project for a 'New European Order' was defeated by overwhelming force of arms. The victorious powers which emerged from the Second World War rejected the ideas underlying the Nazi's New European Order and the experience of the struggle to defeat the Nazis biased them against both separatism and irredentism.

JUSTIFICATIONS OF IMPERIAL RULE

One form of separatism in the post-1945 period had the approval of both the USA and the USSR, as well as progressive opinion in Europe – the emancipation of the territories of the old European colonial empires of France, Britain, Netherlands, and eventually of Spain and Portugal. Nationalism was considered a progressive and liberalising force in the specific context of colonial possessions. Nationalist movements fighting for emancipation of their peoples sought to invent a national consciousness and a united people to replace societies fragmented into tribes, castes, religions and parochial loyalties. Britain eventually preferred to deal with nationalist movements in order to secure, as far as possible, a stable transition from imperial rule to independence. Although homage was generally paid by the international community to the principle of self-determination, the influence of the major powers was placed more behind two other principles enunciated in the Charter of the United Nations – the outlawing of aggression and non-interference in the affairs of other states. These, in practice, conflicted with the right of self-determination.

After the Second World War, major powers no longer tried to seize more territory. They tried to extend their influence through alliances, client states and satellite states. American leadership over the 'free world' was sometimes called 'the American Empire' but it was unlike empires throughout history which had imposed direct rule on other peoples. American administrations were explicitly opposed to such imperialist practices. The Soviet Union had more parallels with traditional empires, but these were not generally recognised until the Soviet hegemony collapsed. In the course of the Second World War Russia had seized the Baltic states of Estonia, Latvia and Lith-uania, a large slice of Polish territory, and smaller areas from Czechoslovakia and Romania. These were all reacquisitions of territory which had at one time been part of the Tsarist Empire. The only new territorial acquisition by the USSR was some of the Kuriles Islands from Japan, which remain a source of tension between the two countries. In extending its influence into Central Europe, the Soviet leaders were content to exercise control through satellite regimes rather than annex territory.

In the foreign policies of both the USA and the USSR there was considerable hypocrisy in their adherence to the principles of the United Nations. Both engaged in interference in the internal affairs of other states and were prepared to condone aggression when their interests were at stake (see Chapter 1). All aggressive acts were blamed on the behaviour of the other. Thus the Berlin blockade of 1949 was a retaliatory measure, according to Moscow, for the moves towards the restoration of a unified German government in the western zones of occupation. The Korean war of 1950–54 was blamed by both sides on the aggressive moves of the other, although the evidence now available demonstrates conclusively it was a war of aggress-ion by North Korea with the connivance of both Mao and Stalin. Claims on other people's territory and overt aggression seemed to be so tarnished by the behaviour of the Axis powers that they were no longer publicly made even by powers which espoused revolutionary principles.

Despite the new climate, colonial powers deployed various arguments to justify retention of overseas territories. In the immediate aftermath of the Second World War, France asserted her title to sovereignty, when faced by revolts in Algeria, Madagascar and Indo-China. In due course, three lines of defence, in addition to the claim to be the legitimate sovereign authority, for French imperial rule emerged. The first was the 'defence of the West' – of French/European/sometimes Christian civilisation and values against new forms of barbarism. The second was that some of the French colonies were constitutionally part of France and that France could not leave them without destroying national unity. This was a principle introduced to the constitution of the French Union of 1946, widely regarded in France as a great benefit to the overseas indigenous elites, and one that would bind them to France. The third type of defence used the rhetoric of self-determination – the colonial peoples would clearly decide to stay with France if they could decide their fate freely without the intimidation of Soviet-supported agitators.

All three forms of defence, which met with increased scepticism in France and abroad, are based on a nationalist assumption that the French nation is an elite nation. Although the defence of the West, a commonplace in right-wing circles, was couched in terms of the defence of European civilisation, the French were assumed to be the vanguard, and the most developed form, of European civilisation. The second suggested that the colonial peoples could be integrated and assimilated into France, and that most of them would willingly do so because they recognised the benefits of the French language, education, culture and economic progress. The third proposed that the French knew what the colonial peoples wanted or what they would want when 'normality' returned to the territories in which they lived. None of these arguments persuaded the inhabitants of the more populous overseas possessions – although in sub-Saharan Africa and Polynesia some people still believe them and find close association with France attractive.

The British arguments about empire contrasted with the French. Some were genuine imperialists, amongst the most distinguished of whom was Winston Churchill. Most were of an older generation, brought up before the First World War. The imperialist position was that the British empire was the greatest empire which the world had ever seen (however grandiose this claim now seems, it was grounded in fact); the empire demonstrated the British gift for government and for bringing a wide diversity of people from all over the world into a common allegiance to the Crown. This genius for government, developed over of a millennium, represented a tradition and a fund of experience, generally recognised by peoples throughout the empire. The belief in the superiority of the British tradition and British practices was, at least from the second half of the nineteenth century, linked with a sense of racial superiority – the right of the British to rule over 'lesser breeds'. This racism was discredited after the Second World War, but continued in rather pathetic extremist groups like the League of Empire Loyalists.

The British colonial administration was believed to have a responsibility to bring the benefits of British justice and administration to the colonised peoples. This contention was shared by the 'pure' imperialists who thought the empire should be retained and 'liberal' imperialists who believed that imperial rule was a trust which should be relinquished when colonial peoples were ready for self-government. The latter became the dominant view during and after the Second World War. The problem was that only the imperial power was in a position to decide when the indigenous peoples were suff-iciently politically educated to be allowed self rule. This maturity would be demonstrated when, in the view of the colonial administration and the British government, the colonial peoples could run a 'Westminster model' of parlia-mentary government.

Britain's global responsibilities were also thought to be a justification for holding on to colonies and military bases. 'Global responsibilities' was a blanket term for the defence of legitimate interests – for example, in secur-ing oil supplies, maintaining world peace by being in a position to help, within a system of collective security, to resist aggressive regimes, and, in a general way, promoting global stability by not leaving a power vacuum in sensitive areas. Other countries could not be trusted, or trusted to the same extent as Britain, to maintain global peace and stability.

The nationalist assumptions of the British and French arguments in favour of imperial rule are very clear in retrospect. They were less clear before these empires were liquidated because imperial 'responsibilities' seemed pressing realities. The withdrawal from empire appeared to be an abandon-ment of responsibilities in two senses – first, it risked creating situations of international instability and war; second, without proper preparation, there were grave risks that some of the colonised peoples could not run a modern state, and large areas would descend into anarchy. There was some foundation to both of these anxieties. What is more certain is that the nationalisms of the imperial powers provoked nationalisms of the colonised peoples, and that the latter gained majority sympathy from third countries.

THE SPREAD OF NATIONALISM

The nationalism of the peoples of black Africa, India and elsewhere was often represented as the result of the intellectual influence, transmitted by the schools and universities, of strands of thinking in Britain and France. The London School of Economics (LSE) and the Left bank of the Seine stood accused of disseminating doctrines which destroyed the foundations of imperial rule. But there were a whole series of sources from which the colonised peoples could draw inspiration to contest imperial rule – aspects of Christianity, particularly Protestantism, contractarian political theory, the Enlightenment, the American Declaration of Independence, the ideas of the French Revolution, nineteenth-century liberalism, Marxism and even racism could be turned on its head to place the white imperialists lower in the natural order than non-white peoples. The political strength of nationalism is that it could use a diversity of themes to strengthen its appeal and adapt it to a wide variety of circumstances.

African and Indian nationalism had parallels with East European nationalisms because they shared one common circumstance – they were confronted with ethnic diversity (and often cultural and religious diversity as well) in the territories which they sought to control. Religious tensions caused a chain reaction which led to a partition of British India, into India and Pakistan. But both these countries contained within their boundaries a diversity of languages, religions, peoples and relics of old political systems. In the African case, if ethnic criteria had been used to define territory, at least ten times as many as the fifty-one states which emerged from colonial rule would have been established; the old colonial boundaries cut across at least 187 'tribal territories'. Ethnic nationalism was not an option in these circumstances. The Indian and African nationalists therefore set out to create nations which previously did not exist. As in Eastern Europe, nationalism was a political project to unify societies, make them defensible and set them on the path to developing modern economies. The strong link between 'modernisation' and nationalism, suggested by Ernest Gellner, has considerable plausibility for both East European and anti-colonial nationalism.

Post-colonial nationalism had considerable success in keeping countries together. In both the Indian subcontinent and Africa, irredentist and separatist crises have occurred. Only two separatist movements have succeeded – Eritrea and Bangladesh – and major ones have failed. Kashmir remains a large disputed territory but there have been only minor territorial revisions between states. The building of new nations within these boundaries of the old colonial territories had varying degrees of success; in certain parts of sub-Saharan Africa it has failed in the face of social disintegration and violence. But alternatives to the old colonial divisions, based on variants of nationalism such as pan-Africanism and pan-Arabism, have, like their virtually forgotten predecessor, pan-Slavism, completely failed. The 'nation-state' has remained the only attractive model for the relatively poor former colonies and dependencies.

The end of the old colonial empires threatened to reduce a certain intermingling of peoples. 'Africanisation' and its equivalents removed the white elites from privileged positions in the former colonies and their numbers dropped very quickly. The old imperial powers put up immigration controls against people from their old colonial possessions. Educational links continued but some atrophied because of lack of resources, nationalist reticences and declining commitment. The nation-state model in general divided, at least temporarily, the whole world into separate sovereignties, with distinctive national loyalties, interests and citizenship. The gain seemed to be that the political map of the world was settling down. The governments of states had to be content with the territory and peoples whom they controlled, because the international system was strongly biased against separatism and irredentism. The costs involved in challenging the status quo were great and the chances of success small. Iraq has, for example, paid a very high price for its irredentist claim for, and invasion of, Kuwait; the legitimacy of Israel's hold on occupied territories is constantly challenged; the twenty-five-year attempt of Indonesia to annex East Timor failed.

CONTEMPORARY IRREDENTIST ISSUES

The promise of territorial stability was thrown into question by the events in the Balkans and Eastern Europe, following the events of 1989, when a re-renewed nationalism seemed to prefigure another period of conflict over territory. Once again complexity of the ethnic map made possible irredentist and separatist claims. No confident judgement is yet possible on the permanence of the present territorial settlement. Ernest Gellner (1997), in an interesting if simplified way, explained the basis of the current instability. He divides Europe into four zones. The first is the Atlantic seaboard of Europe where strong dynastic states, established before the age of nationalism, successfully brought together the boundaries of culture and state. London, Lisbon, Madrid and Paris ruled territories which had a certain linguistic-cultural homogeneity. With the high tide of nationalism, there was no need to change frontiers very much to make cultural frontiers coincide with state frontiers. The only new state to emerge as a result of nationalism in this zone was Ireland – Norway separated from Sweden in 1905 but it had been independent before 1814.

In the second zone just to the east, common cultures existed before states were created which represented them. Italy, since Dante and the early Renaissance, had a language and a cultural patrimony, shared by elites throughout the peninsula. Germany since Luther in the sixteenth century, and even before, when the Teutonic knights pushed towards the east, had developed a common literary language capable of serving as the basis of a culturally homogeneous zone. Political fragmentation characterised this area until the mid-nineteenth century. In the age of nationalism, unification of these culturally homogeneous zones became a burning ambition of nationalist activists. In both, Gellner argues, 'nationalism could be both benign and liberal; it had no inherent need to go nasty (even if in the end it did)'.

This contrasts with the third zone where nationalism was bound to have unpleasantly violent implications – Eastern Europe where in the nineteenth century there were neither national states nor national cultures. If the nineteenth-century imperative of one state, one culture was to be followed, both states and cultures had to be created. The states which existed were only loosely connected with their own dominant ethnic group. Frequently members of other ethnic groups held powerful positions both in state and society. National states had to be established in an area of complicated ethnic mixtures and national cultures had to be invented. Especially in the Balkans, the Caucasus and the Volga bend, homogeneous national states could only be created by transfer of populations or what has come to be known as 'ethnic cleansing'.

Within this third zone a fourth zone exists – the area which was under communist control for between forty and seventy years. Of the three empires which had dominated Central and Eastern Europe prior to 1914, one, the Russian, was reconstituted in a particularly ruthless and murderous form. Gellner suggests, controversially, that it was a non-nationalist dominium and it certainly had no difficulty in suppressing lesser nationalisms. But nationalism, which was not the cause of its collapse according to Gellner, profited from its demise with the result that weak, inexperienced states, troubled by minority questions, have emerged in its wake. In this fourth zone, separatist movements and irredentist claims are inevitable unless or until a profound transformation of these societies takes place.

This scenario identifies the problems of Eastern Europe as specific to the region. The separatist and irredentist claims in which West European powers have been involved since the end of Empire have been trivial by comparison. Belgium, a relatively new state (founded 1930), is a possible exception, but there is no wish by neighbouring states to take over parts of the country, should it disintegrate. Britain is the power most involved in irredentist claims. Two in recent years can be regarded as the left-overs of empire – Hong Kong and the Falkland Islands – with Gibraltar and Northern Ireland presenting different problems. In all, except Hong Kong, where political calculation about the possible reaction of the People's Republic of China determined otherwise, Britain took its stand firmly on the principle of self-determination.

In the case of Gibraltar and the Falklands the populations were tiny; Gibraltar has just over 30,000, two-thirds of whom are Gibraltarian citizens of a British dependent territory; in the case of the Falklands the population of just over 2,000 have the same status. The size of these populations allowed

Spain and Argentina to question whether the principle of self-determination was being used as a pretext to maintain an imperial presence. In Northern Ireland the claim made by the Republic of Ireland in articles 2 and 3 of its 1949 Constitution for the whole of the island of Ireland was not pressed by the Irish governments in any active way. But a militant minority in Northern Ireland has opposed British sovereignty over the province since 1969. A majority of about two-thirds of the population of Northern Ireland is firmly of the view that the status quo is desirable. Scottish and Welsh nationalist parties are separatist parties which do not wish to change the borders of their countries. The separatist threats to Spain in the Basque country and Catalunya, and to France in Corsica, although troublesome, have been of lesser intensity and are unlikely to result in the fragmentation of these states. None of these problems are on the scale or intensity of those found in Eastern Europe.

THE 'FRAYING' OF THE FRONTIERS OF THE NATION-STATES?

In Europe, is there any other way in which new national identities and new nationalisms could emerge? In the short term this seems unlikely but the long term could change. John Herz described, almost forty years ago, the breaking down of 'the hard shell' of the nation-state.[33] The reasons for this, mainly associated with the processes of Europeanisation and globalisation, are discussed in the next chapter. Frontiers no longer mark lines of military defence and in the European Union they are no longer barriers to the movement of people, goods, capital, services and information. In this context, the development of transfrontier cooperation between local and regional authorities, private associations and economic interests has acquired a new significance.

The first forms of transfrontier cooperation between local governments (across the Rhine) originated in the early 1950s as part of a movement for Franco-German reconciliation. The enthusiasm for building bridges between people formerly effectively sealed off by frontiers has been reproduced in different circumstances in different places – on the French–Spanish frontier after the restoration of democracy in Spain and at the eastern frontier of the EU after the collapse of communism; the enthusiasm wanes in course of time but the arrangements for cooperation remain in place.

In the early 1960s, the focus of transfrontier cooperation in the core areas of Western Europe changed from reconciliation between peoples to overcoming difficulties created by the international frontier for economic development, particularly in the field of land-use planning. For example, the requirements of the Basel economy and the lack of suitable room for expansion in Switzerland prompted the setting up of a planning office, the *Regio Basiliensis*, which analysed the infrastructure and labour market requirements for the wider Basel region, including southern Alsace in France and the southwest corner of Baden Württemberg in Germany. Many other examples in widely separated European frontier regions of practical cooperation in economic matters emerged in the 1960s.

In the aftermath of the protest movements of the 1960s a new concern about the environment emerged leading to direct action campaigns, pressure groups and green parties. This affected the agenda of transfrontier cooperation and, in some places, exhibited a genuine popular basis leading to concrete results. The mobilisation of opposition against the concentration of nuclear power stations on the upper Rhine in the 1970s, the Lake Constance Conference which saved the Lake from environmental catastrophe, and other examples in Saar-Lorraine-Luxembourg, the Danube and the Alpine regions showed the vitality of the environmentalist movement. This is particularly significant because it is a clear example of the 'bottom up' pressure to engage in transfrontier cooperation, contrasting with the previous approach of elite cooperation.

In the second half of the 1970s, and for part of the 1980s (a period described as one of 'Euro-scelerosis' or 'Euro-stagnation'), promoters of European integration took an interest in transfrontier cooperation. This helped to infuse cooperation with a new sense of purpose at a time when the standing and influence of land-use planners was in decline. Cooperation acquired a treaty basis in the Madrid Convention of 1980 which has subsequently been strengthened by a protocol and bilateral treaties negotiated between neighbouring states. In the period since the 1985 Single European Act, hardnosed material interests have come to the fore – there has been a need for the economic development of frontier regions, new opportunities for joint ventures emerged with the dismantling of the frontier controls and, above all, there was the prospect of EU financial aid for frontier regions.

Transfrontier cooperation looks set to flourish, particularly in areas such as the Baltic where there are widespread perceptions of common and interrelated problems which cannot be tackled without it. This cooperation suggests, to those in favour of it, that the old sovereign states are fraying at the edges and no longer have complete control over what happens in their own peripheries, thus prefiguring a major diminution of the authority of the nation-state. It is also possible that the experience of working together, the development of a community of interests and habitual ways of doing things will create new territorial identities. These territorial identities could emerge, sometimes on the basis of ones which have once existed – the Rhineland, the *Kaisertreue* Habsburg domains, some of the old Hansa towns – with a sense of patriotism and common interest. In the new, more open, fluid European society, the construction of new territorial identities is a possibility.

CONCLUSION

War and nationalism created new states in the nineteenth century, and triggered the disintegration of the multinational empires of Europe – the Habsburg, the Ottoman, the Romanov – at the beginning of the twentieth century. In the middle of the century, the same factors resulted in the disappearance of the old multinational colonial empires of the European powers. The collapse at the end of the century of the multinational states of Yugoslavia, Czechoslovakia and the USSR resulted in a potentially unstable attempt to redraw the political map on the basis of the national principle. Nationalist governments and movements have thus provoked, throughout the twentieth century, territorial disputes through irredentist and separatist demands. The turmoil may be subsiding but we should not fall into the trap of believing that we have reached the end of history. The creation of new territorial identities is possible which will disturb the tranquillity of nation-states whose members complacently think that their frontiers are permanent and unchallengeable realities.

7 Democracy and nationalism

Democratic institutions and practices in the Western liberal countries, for three to four decades following the Second World War, seemed to have little to do with nationalism. Defence of these institutions was occasionally couched in terms which made a link between them and specific forms of national allegiance. Thus, in some cases, the enemies of liberal democracy were not only stigmatised as enemies of freedom but also as alien to the nation. Striking examples of this were the official designation of subversive activities in the United States as 'un-American activities' and de Gaulle's unequivocal dismissal of the French communists as being 'neither of the Right nor the Left but of the East.' But no general relationship between democracy and a sense of national identity was suggested.

Exploration of the general link between ideas of the nation and democracy has reemerged in the last two decades of the twentieth century following some of the developments discussed in previous chapters. The ending of the Cold War, the search for new bases of political legitimacy, the new claims on behalf of small nations, globalisation and European integration, concerns about immigration and multiculturalism have led to discussions of the nature of majority rule and the reasons why people accept it. The question has been raised but the precise connections between liberal democracy, national identity and nationalism are a theoretical and historical conundrum.

THE HISTORICAL BACKGROUND

An historical connection can be made between the spread of representative democracy and the rise of nationalism in the nineteenth century, despite the frequent mobilisation of nationalist ideas in the twentieth century to destroy democracy. One basic premise of nationalism laid the foundation for the spread of democratic rule. This is that everyone belonged to a nation and, by this very fact, enjoyed certain rights and privileges. The implication was not necessarily that people enjoyed democratic rights but belonging to a nation meant that all (at least male) citizens were, in some sense, equal. Under the old order people enjoyed collective feudal rights as members of an aristocratic military caste, as clergy or as burghers (with the majority of the population in a servile relationship to these estates). This *ancien regime* was undermined by a series of factors – centralising monarchies, religious wars, the expansion of Europe into other regions which provided means of escape for individuals, the growing importance of trade from the fourteenth to the eighteenth century, and the beginnings of industrial society. Nationalism struck a fatal blow at the old order because belonging to a nation altered the focus of loyalty and the basis of political legitimacy.

Feudal assumptions persisted within the new industrialising and democratising world of the nineteenth and early twentieth centuries, and the mentalities associated with 'estates' remained influential within virtually all European societies until they were effectively destroyed by the two World Wars. In the atypical case of the United Kingdom, remnants of the society of estates survived after 1945, with an upper house of parliament composed of hereditary peers, judges and bishops of the established Church. This remnant of the pre-modern world was linked to the hereditary monarchy and represented an idea of historical continuity which had become part of the core of British national identity. But British 'exceptionalism' is changing. At the symbolic level, the hereditary principle embodied in the House of Lords has come to be regarded by a large majority of public opinion as inappropriate in the contemporary world where the political and legal equality of individuals seems self-evident.

In the rapidly changing, large societies of the nineteenth century, where class, caste and corporate loyalties were weakening, the creation of a social bond was a pressing practical problem. Mobilising populations to defend vigorously states and institutions of self-government, where these latter existed, was an urgent necessity for many politicians. Common membership of a nation, because it could be based on some previously existing commitments, provided a sufficiently strong bond. The strength of this bond was particularly evident in two World Wars of the twentieth century. For liberals and democrats this common membership had certain implications. To deny rights to some members of the nation, which others enjoyed, and to give some people privileged access to government by right of birth could only be justified by very special reasons. In the nineteenth century, these reasons could be that some sections of society were too poor or too ill-educated to exercise rights responsibly but, for the liberal nationalist, these circumstances could and ought to change over time.

The extension of the right to vote in parliamentary elections in the nineteenth century, until it became universal suffrage in the twentieth century, is historically associated with nationalism. Conservatives, such as Disraeli, thought of the granting of the vote as binding broader sections of the population into the nation. The connection between democratic ideas and the nation was most clearly made by the nineteenth-century liberal thinker, John Stuart Mill. He firmly believed that 'the question of government ought to be decided by the governed' but that 'free institutions were next to impossible in states made up of different nationalities'.[34] A common loyalty, ease of communication between members of a society, and shared values were, for liberals, the essential basis for democratic participation and the stability of democratic institutions. The underlying liberal assumption was that the basic identity of any population was the nation and that, within multinational states, loyalties to nations would create barriers to communication and unmanageable conflict. Liberals who reject nationalism nonetheless usually believe that an enduring sense of community provides the civic virtues necessary for free and fair elections, representative government and the rule of law. Anti-nationalist liberals have not yet invented a plausible alternative to the sense of belonging provided by a common membership of the nation.

John Stuart Mill, along with Renan, Durkheim and many nineteenth-century thinkers, suggested that a shared past was the most important bond of a nation. As Renan wrote:

> The strongest cause of a feeling of nationality ... is identity of political antecedents; the possession of a national history, and consequent community of recollections; collective pride and humiliation, pleasure and regret, connected with the same incidents in the past.[35]

This assumes a reasonable knowledge of history or even of an erroneous version of history, fervently believed, on the part of citizens. Support for another great nineteenth-century innovation – universal education – was shared by all liberal nationalists. Whether Mill's assumption still holds in face of what has been called the disappearance of the past (the lack of knowledge and interest in the past by the majority of citizens in the late twentieth century) may be open to question. The efforts made by governments, through support for national heritage or patrimony, to rectify this, and to recreate a sense of a common past indicates the perceived political importance of this.

CHALLENGES TO NATIONALISM

During the high tide of nationalism in the late nineteenth and early twentieth centuries, there were challenges to the view that the nation is the primary source of loyalty and political legitimacy. These challenges provide some clues to answering questions about whether plausible alternatives to the nation can be invented. People across the political spectrum in the nineteenth century rejected the national principle on a variety of grounds. Some of these challenges held that democracy was either impossible or undesirable or both. Legitimists who believed in a hereditary monarchy and ultramontane Catholics who believed in the primacy of the spiritual authority of the Pope over temporal rulers refused to accept that the basis of political power was the people and continued to hold that political authority was divinely ordained. Traditionalists held that the most secure basis of political authority was to follow precedents handed down from the past and modify them only when compelled by circumstances to do so.

At the other end of the political spectrum, the most extreme exponents of the principle of 'power to the people' were not democrats in the liberal meaning of the term. Anarchists, anarcho-syndicalists and Marxist socialists all considered that the national principle was usually a tool used by an exploiting class or oppressive elites. Marx and Engels wrote, in the Communist Manifesto of 1848, that 'the working man has no country'. Although this is not the most perceptive remark they made about nationalism, it is the best remembered. Closer to the mainstream of British political life, a liberal pluralist such as Lord Acton held the view that a multinational state was an assurance of liberty, a barrier against autocracy because it required a dispersal of political power. In his view, it was the failure of rulers of multinational states to recognise the necessity of dispersal of power, rather than the inevitable victory of the national idea, which caused the disintegration of these states.

The First World War period produced a new and serious ideological challenge to nationalism for the first time since the 1848 breakdown of the dynastically based European order, known as the Metternich system. An overtly internationalist revolution destroyed the old Imperial order in Russia in 1917 and threatened to spread to Hungary, Germany and Italy in the immediate aftermath of the War. The likelihood of a successful communist revolution spreading throughout Europe quickly faded but the 'spectre of communism haunted' inter-war Europe more seriously than it had when Marx and Engels had coined the phrase in the Communist Manifesto of 1848. The fear of communism helped to bring to power nationalist right-wing dictatorships in most of the southern and east central European countries. The best known of these was Mussolini's fascist dictatorship in Italy.

Communism was not the only challenge to nationalism. A liberal internationalism, which rejected nationalism and proposed constraints on the sovereignty of nation-states, gained support among political elites. After the First World War, liberal internationalism was mainly expressed by backing the League of Nations and the first influential proposals for a European Union. This liberal internationalism was, however, ambivalent because it was also associated with the right of self-determination of peoples. This right asserted a strong link between nationalism and democracy if the exercise of self-determination was associated with free and fair elections and entrenched rights for minorities. But it could be interpreted in an authoritarian and undemocratic way – that people with certain objective characteristics in common (language and culture) should be assigned to the same state. This was the interpretation of the Nazis – even though they had overwhelming popular support for the annexation of the Sudeten and Austria.

The Second World War strengthened the rhetoric and the institutions of liberal internationalism. The experience of this war provided the basis of a challenge, both at the global and regional levels, to the absolute sovereignty of the state. This challenge was that states should be required to cooperate to promote international peace and stability, prosperity, and justice. Specifically, liberal internationalists proposed that states should be bound by rules of good behaviour towards each other by refraining from aggression and interference in others' internal affairs. In a proposal which conflicted with the principle of non-interference, liberal internationalists also held that states should be bound by rules of good behaviour towards their own citizens. These rules were expressed in practice by the League of Nations' sponsored minorities treaties in the inter-war period and by the 1948 Universal Declaration of Human Rights, other post-Second-World-War agreements such as the UN Convention on Genocide and the 1976 Covenants on civic, political, economic and social rights.

In the post-Second-World-War world liberal internationalism became part of a project to divorce democratic institutions from ideas of the nation and regard representative and responsible government as part of the common patrimony of the 'free world'. Free elections, the rule of law and human rights were of universal applicability. A notion of cosmopolitan citizenship was developed according to which everyone enjoyed certain rights as members of the human race. Liberal internationalists thought of nationalism as based on a primitive, irrational fear of the foreigner and it was inextricably linked to its most extreme expressions – Nazism and Fascism. These ideas became widely adopted; they became a kind of conventional wisdom among the Western democracies.

In some circles, including the realist school of international relations, liberal internationalism was considered empty rhetoric. Reality, in this meaning of 'realism', is that the international system is an anarchical society in which the states in practice still retain absolute power within their territories, and enjoy freedom of action externally, insofar as their size, resources and armaments allow. One of the main reasons for the continuing authority of the state in the post-1945 world, realists and others argued, was the loyalty of their populations and this loyalty, however described, is based on forms of nationalism. Close to this position are those who believe that the nation and national identity are the only defences against oppressive imperialism. Some of those who have adopted this position, like the French Minister of the Interior (1997–) Jean-Pierre Chévènement, have regarded concern about human rights, in Bosnia, Kosovo, China and elsewhere, as a cover for American imperialism.

The attempt to escape from nationalism and the national bond produced some intellectually sophisticated ideas. One was the invention of the notion of 'political culture' as the foundation of democracy. An influential text in Western social science, *The Civic Culture* (1963) by G. A. Almond and S. Verba, made this concept widely known. It characterised political culture as 'attitudes toward the political system and its various parts, and attitudes towards the role of the self in the system'. When Gabriel Almond returned to the topic almost twenty years later (in G. A. Almond and S. Verba eds, *The Civic Culture Re-Visited* [1981]) he wrote that the 'concept stressed political knowledge and skill, and feelings and value orientations towards political objects and processes – toward the political system as a whole, toward self as a participant, toward political parties and elections, bureaucracy and the like'.

Some political cultures supported democratic practices, whilst others did not. Almond and Verba identified three main types of political culture. First, the parochial political culture in which there are no specialised political roles, no separation of these from religious and social roles and there is no expectation of change from the political system. This is a type of political culture present in primitive and tribal societies but it is also to be found in some larger ones such as the Ottoman Empire. The second is the subject political culture in which individuals are aware of the characteristics of the state and the policies of government; they may even approve of them but they do not think that there is anything effective they can do to affect political outcomes. Italy in the 1950s was in this category, with an alienated political culture in which there was a virtually complete absence of trust between citizens and political authorities. Third is the participant political culture in which there is a good level of knowledge about the political system, the political authorities have a high degree of legitimacy and citizens believe that they can affect political outcomes.

The third kind is clearly superior to the first two. The implication was that, with growing prosperity and the right kind of civic education, it could spread to other societies making them more like the Anglo-American model of a participatory democracy. This concept of political culture has been very influential, although highly controversial, because it suggested that the culture present in a society explained the characteristics of the political system. The problem with this attempted escape from nationalism is that the characteristics necessary to support democracy could well be described, by liberal nationalists, as national characteristics.

CONTEMPORARY ISSUES

The basis of support, and to what extent national identity is crucial, for democratic institutions is of great contemporary significance. The answer depends on whether existing multinational states such as Canada and India can survive as democratic polities and whether new regional groupings, such as the European Union, can have a genuinely democratic basis. Whether the United Kingdom can survive if, in a part of the kingdom, being Scottish rather than British is regarded as the national identity. Whether Corsica can remain within the French state if Corsicans become convinced that they are different and subject to separate and unequal treatment from the French state. At other levels, can the European Union rectify its 'democratic deficit' and evolve into a genuinely democratic federation without a sense of European nationhood? World 'government' seems a functional requirement to manage major economic turbulence and prevent ecological disaster. Can a new loyalty to the 'common interest of mankind' be constructed to support new global regimes?

Three themes raise doubts about democracy breaking out of the national framework – the omnipresence of national symbols in everyday life; the appeals made by politicians to national sentiment; the relative failure of international institutions to mobilise popular enthusiasm. None of these suggest that other bases of support for democratic institutions are impossible to establish, but they do suggest great difficulties in doing so. The first is concerned with what Michael Billig has memorably described as banal nationalism – not to be confused with benign or harmless nationalism, because it can be associated with aggressive and authoritarian nationalism. Banal nationalism is the use of visual images and recurrent phrases to remind people of their common membership of the nation and their loyalty to it.

Banal nationalism is exemplified by the routines of remembering, and selectively forgetting, the national past, which pass without notice in the well-established democracies of the rich countries. In these democracies the national flag is ever present. Ritual occasions such as national holidays, some with military parades, others with evocations of a founding myth of the nation, or in the case of the United Kingdom, the Royal Christmas broadcast, remind the population, in a routine way, of belonging to a national community. The prowess of national sporting teams is a supreme example of benign nationalism. Sporting victories are routinely represented as national triumphs and are celebrated as such – when France won the World Cup in 1998 well in excess of two million people thronged the streets of Paris. Many of those interviewed on television claimed that they had no interest at all in football. Other countries are identified by their flags and symbols when actions of their leaders are reported. In international organisations, states are labelled by their national flags. Newspaper and television journalists, by a series of commonly used phrases, identify 'us' and the 'others'. These indications of national identity, as Michael Billig says, seem to occur everywhere once one starts to look.

The second theme can be abundantly illustrated. Democratically elected politicians give daily evidence that they consider that both national symbols and the explicit appeal to national sentiments are important in mobilising support. The Conservative Party, conforming to a pattern of parties throughout the world, never fails to feature the Union Jack prominently at party conferences and frequently on its election literature. Explicit references to the nation and even the outdated notion of 'national character' are a recurrent theme in electoral and other appeals for public support. The Conservatives who took Britain into the European Community – Harold Macmillan and Edward Heath – never failed to mention Great Britain, the virtues of the nation and the national interest. This rhetoric has continued to seem an essential part of a successful politician's repertoire, as Prime Minister Blair exemplifies.

Similarly, in France anxiety about a decline of the national bond and the implications of this for democracy is acute, because of the founding principles of the French State. The 1789 Declaration of the Rights of Man (which forms part of the preamble to the current Constitution) states 'the principle of all sovereignty resides essentially in the nation. No body, no individual can exercise any authority which is not expressly issued by it.' In the face of ethnic claims, regional assertiveness, the authority of the European Union and perhaps, above all, a liberal individualism in which economic interests are given priority over civic virtue, the very basis of a French conception of democracy seems at risk. In the opinion of some members of the French elite, there no longer seems to be the will to defend democratic institutions. As Dominique Schnapper has eloquently put it: 'In a democracy there is no longer any sense of supreme sacrifice: individuals and their interests have replaced the citizens and their principles.'[36]

The third theme is that attempts to establish democratic procedures, which transcend the national context, have not been notably successful despite the proliferation of international institutions and the growth of international non-governmental organisations. There is no method, at the moment, by which electorates can express their preferences for choices at the global level. Support for organisations concerned with global humanitarian aims (Oxfam, *Médecins sans Frontières* and many others) and environmental aims (Greenpeace, World Wildlife Watch) suggests a significant commitment on the part of active minorities. But there is no demand for a world parliament and no obvious way in which it could be efficiently established. Also, there is a lack of emotional attachment to global and European institutions. A concrete example of this lack of an equivalent commitment to European democratic procedures is shown in the voting turnout in European elections. Between 1979, when direct elections started, and 1999, voter turnout declined from 63 percent to 47 percent despite an increase in powers of the European Parliament and European institutions in general after the entry into force of the Treaty of Amsterdam.

IS THE LINK BETWEEN NATIONALISM AND DEMOCRACY UNDESIRABLE?

A new debate has commenced in the 1990s emphasising that national identity is necessary to democracy. David Miller starts his study of nationality by stating that, although many regard this as unfortunate: 'The claims of nationality have come to dominate politics in the last decade of the twentieth century.' Miller, and other liberal nationalists, admit that there is a tendency to identify nationalism with the less secure, more aggressive assertions of national identity in poorer countries, especially in dictatorships where national sentiment seems to be manipulated to keep regimes in power. Nationalism has been, and is, regarded as monstrous, inefficient and tyrannical leading to ethnic genocide, imperialism, blood-letting and denial of human rights. Nationalism also seems to give overwhelming priority to the needs of the national group and brushes aside personal fulfilment and individual rights.

But Miller, with others who have contributed to the debate in the 1990s such as Neil MacCormick, Tom Nairn, Yael Tamir and Dominique Schnapper, mounted a powerful liberal defence of the national idea and its importance in sustaining democratic institutions. They all take the view that national identities change over time and that they are not immutable elements of human nature but, they argue, they are desirable and, in the present context, irreplaceable. Miller forcibly argues that national identity is a proper part of personal identity, that nations are ethical communities and that members of nations owe more duties to fellow nationals than to non-nationals, and that a national community on a given territory has a good claim to self-determination. This does not necessarily mean a sovereign state – for MacCormick the sovereign state is in any case now an outdated concept. Supranational institutions and local autonomies are both possible within the terms of liberal nationalism.

The arguments of the liberal nationalists are subtle and far-reaching. In general they share a concept of the nation as a cultural community formed by many things – a shared history, a language, a literature and other artistic forms, mythology and folklore, religion and law, and educational institutions. Individuals feel, to varying extents but usually strongly, that their national identity is part of their personal identity. All these things which help to support the legitimacy of governments are part of what it is to be a nation. There are important disagreements from this starting point – for Dominique Schnapper, drawing on an influential French tradition, nations are inseparable from political units or states. But Yael Tamir and Neil MacCormick are particularly insistent that nations should not be confused with states and it is the identification of state and nation which has potentially anti-liberal implications. The reality of nations, for Tamir and MacCormick, has political implications because it creates the aspiration to self-government. This aspiration is admirable because it allows the personal fulfilment of individuals.

These liberal nationalists are aware of the danger of zealous or extreme nationalism. They argue, however, that despotism, political horrors, persecutions and hatred of foreigners existed before the nation-state and they are not the monopoly of nationalists. Tom Nairn argues that the horrors associated with imperial rule are much worse than those of national self-rule. Liberal nationalists also argue that an undemocratic nation-state is a perversion because it denies its population of the right to self-rule. This is not, therefore, a legitimate form of government because the people cannot feel that the institutions of the state are 'theirs'.

CONCLUSION

Several grounds have been advanced in this chapter for a relationship between democratic institutions and national sentiments. Amongst these are the historical and conceptual link between nationalist and democratic ideas, the beliefs of contemporary politicians, the arguments of distinguished sociologists like Schnapper, the empirical studies of nationalism, the low turnout in European elections, the reality of national cultures. These do not prove that there is a link. But they create a strong presumption that such a link has existed and continues to exist.

Whether there is a necessary connection between the two is much less certain. Indeed there seems no reason in principle that democratic institutions are impossible in the absence of a national bond. But something would have to replace it. At a minimum, democracy means self-rule and this is difficult to envisage without bounded communities for some purposes of government. How those boundaries should be drawn and what could hold people together within them in loyal support of democratic procedures in the absence of a national bond is not, at the moment, obvious. This does not mean such a state of affairs will not happen. A European *demos* – a multinational 'people' or a sense of global solidarity – may emerge which will provide the basis of loyalty and trust necessary for democracy.

Conclusion

General assessments of the impact of nationalism and the meaning of national identity involve 'big questions, large processes, huge comparisons'.[37] Such assessments are personal and cannot claim general validity. There are bound to be disagreements about them.

Nonetheless, some propositions about nationalism are clearly false. In this category are the early twentieth-century beliefs – that nationalism is a force of nature, omnipresent, permanent and self-evidently true. Towards the end of the century other prevalent views of nationalism are equally false – nationalism is a fallacious set of beliefs, an infantile disorder ('the measles of the human race' as Albert Einstein described it), and dead or dying.

Nationalism has been modified over the last century. It is no longer the phenomenon Norman Angell described in 1932: 'Political nationalism has become for the European of our age, the most important thing in the world, more important than, civilisation, humanity, kindness, piety; more important than life itself.'[38] For some – militant Irish or Basque nationalists, some people in ex-Yugoslavia and parts of the former Soviet Union – nationalism still has this potency. In the countries of the European Union, and those who aspire to join it, nationalist passions have diminished despite the attempts of some extreme Right groups to revive them.

A long period without armed conflict in Europe, the growth of European and global institutions, the flourishing of international non-governmental organisations, technological changes which have made the world a smaller place and greater awareness of the world beyond national boundaries have made the grand simplicities of the early twentieth century, encapsulated by the phrase 'my country right or wrong', much less prevalent at the end of the twentieth century. Other interests and values, some of which complement, others which conflict with national allegiances, have modified the content of the national identity of the peoples of Europe. The content and nature of these national identities is also much better understood as a result of theoretical works such as that of David Miller and empirical work such as that of Uwe Hedetoft.

The recent debate in social science and political theory on nationalism has resulted in a more balanced view of the phenomenon. There is less of a tendency to regard patriotism as good and nationalism as bad or to divide nationalism itself into good and bad categories, which was a characteristic of an older generalisation of scholars.[39] There are varieties of nationalism and the nationalism of each people has unique features. If some take a virulent form, it is not because of the intrinsic wickedness or perversity of nationalist doctrines in general but has much to do with the structural characteristics of societies and the nature of particular conflicts. Beliefs in the vital importance of national identity also support liberal democratic institutions in the context of wealthy, relatively homogeneous societies.

Arguments that national identities are eroding under the pressure of Europeanisation and globalisation are not well-founded. A sense of national identity, as part of personal identity, continues to be a basic feature of European political and social life. National identities are the basis of loyalty to the state. Belief in the benefits of state authority are still strong despite, and up to a point because of, the success of European integration. Global and European institutions do not yet rival the state in terms of loyalties of the vast majority of people. To a degree this is because the state provides highly valued security and public services, either by directly controlling them or acting as an agent for the implementation of European policies. But it is also because states are expressions, and promoters, of national identities. Where there are significant challenges to existing states, as in Scotland, these are based on competing national identities.

The present role and impact of nationalism is not the end point of historical development. The words of Durkheim, written at the beginning of the twentieth century, still apply: 'The more evolution advances and the more one sees that the ideal pursued by men is detached from the local and the ethnic, the stronger the conviction becomes that national ends are not at the summit of human development.' His argument continued that the way to reconcile legitimate attachment to the state with universal values is that the civic education given by the state will consist of 'a particular form of general duties owed to the whole of humanity'. Forms of political organisation above and beyond the state can flourish at the same time as states and national identities.[40]

Notes

1 Kedourie, E. (1960, 1993) *Nationalism*, Oxford: Blackwell.
2 Anthony Smith is the most persuasive of contemporary primordialists, and Ernest Gellner of the modernisers. See particularly Smith, A. D. (1986) *The Ethnic Origins of Nations*, Oxford: Blackwell; Gellner, E. (1983) *Nations and Nationalism*, Oxford: Blackwell.
3 In recent years this contrast between German and French views has become misleading with the best known contemporary German philosopher, Habermas, defending a purely civic form of political obligation with his defence of 'constitutional patriotism' – loyalty towards a liberal democratic order takes primacy over any loyalty to a people. White, S. K. (1995) *The Cambridge Companion to Habermas*, Cambridge: Cambridge University Press; Dews, P. (1999) *Habermas: A Critical Reader*, Oxford: Blackwell.
4 Nairn, T. (1997) *Faces of Nationalism: Janus Revisited*, London: Verso; Schnapper, D. (1998) *Community of Citizens; on the Modern Idea of Nationality*, London: Transaction Publishers.
5 Greenfield, L. (1992) *Nationalism: Five Roads to Modernity*, London: Harvard University Press.
6 Anderson, B. (1991) *Imagined Communities: Reflexions on the Origins and Spread of Nationalism*, London: Verso.
7 Plamenatz, J. (1973) 'Two Types of Nationalism' in Kamenka, E. (ed.) *Nationalism: The Nature and Evolution of an Idea*, London: Edward Arnold.
8 Milward, A. (1992) *The European Rescue of the Nation-State*, Berkeley: University of California Press.
9 See Kuisel, R. F. (1993) *Seducing the French: The Dilemma of Americanization*, Berkeley: University of California Press.
10 Billig, M. (1995) *Banal Nationalism*, London: Sage.
11 Zelinsky, W. (1988) *Nation into State: The Shifting Symbolic Functions of American Nationalism*, Chapel Hill: University of North Carolina Press, p. 6.
12 Hofstadter, R. (1979) *The Paranoid Style in American Politics*, Chicago: Chicago University Press.
13 Rogin, M. P. (1988) *Ronald Reagan, the Movie, and other Episodes in Political Demonology*, Chicago: University of Chicago Press.
14 See Walicki, A. (1975) *The Slavophile Controversy*, Oxford: Oxford University Press.
15 For a study of centennial and bicentennial celebrations see Spillman, L. (1997) *Nation and Commemoration: Creating National Identities in the United States and Australia*, Cambridge: Cambridge University Press.
16 The 1945 visit of the emblematic figure of Irish nationalism, Eamon de Valera, to the German embassy to offer condolences on Hitler's death was indicative of narrowness of vision of small nationalisms.

17   Wirth, L. (1945) 'The Problem of Minority Groups' in Linton, R. L. (ed.) *The Science of Man in the World Crisis*, New York: Columbia University Press.
18   Stephens, M. (1976) *Linguistic Minorities in Western Europe*, Llandsuyl: Gomer Press.
19   See the masterly accounts in Weber, E. J. (1977) *Peasants into Frenchmen: the Modernisation of Rural France, 1870–1914*, London: Chatto & Windus; Zeldin, T. (1973, 1977) *France 1848–1945*, 2 vols. Oxford: Clarendon Press and subsequent editions of both works.
20   Hindley, R. (1990) *The Death of the Irish Language: A Qualified Obituary*, London: Routledge.
21   Nairn, T. (1997) *Faces of Nationalism: Janus Revisited*, London: Verso.
22   For an argument that minority nationalism can emerge in all kinds of economic settings see Connor, W. (1984) 'Eco- or Ethno-nationalism?', *Ethics and Racial Studies*, 7, 3, 342–51.
23   Noiriel, G. (1996) *The French Melting Pot: Immigration, Citizenship and National Identity*, Minneapolis: University of Minnesota Press.
24   Milward, A. (1992) *The European Rescue of the Nation State*, Berkeley: University of California Press; Milward, A. and others (1993) *The Frontiers of National Sovereignty: History and Theory 1945–1992*, London: Routledge.
25   Moravcsik, A. (1998) *The Choice for Europe: Social Purpose and State Power from Messina to Maastricht*, Ithaca: Cornell University Press.
26   Young, H. (1998) *This Blessed Plot: Britain and Europe from Churchill to Blair*, London: Macmillan.
27   *Eurobarometer*, March 1999.
28   'It's an interesting test. Are you still harking back to where you came from or where you are?' Marquese, M. (1995) *Anyone but England: Cricket and the National Malaise*, London: Verso.
29   Laqueur, W. (1994) *The Dream that Failed; Reflections on the Soviet Union*, Oxford: Oxford University Press, p. 148.
30   Kennedy, P. M. (1998) *The Rise and Fall of the Great Powers: Economic Change and Military Conflict from 1500 to 1900*, London: Unwin Hyman.
31   Oakeshott, M. (1962) 'Rationalism in Politics' in Oakeshott M. *Rationalism in Politics and Other Essays*, London: University Paperbacks.
32   Fukuyama, F. (1992) *The End of History and the Last Man*, London: Penguin.
33   Herz, J. H. (1961) 'The Rise and Demise of the Territorial State' in Rosenau, J. D. (ed.) *International Politics and Foreign Policy*, New York: Free Press.
34   In his essay on representative government first published in 1861: see Mill, J. S. (1972) *Utilitarianism. On Liberty. Considerations on Representative Government*, London: Dent, p. 392.
35   Renan, E. (1862) 'Qu'est-ce que c'est une nation?' in Renan, E. (1949) *Oeuvres Complètes Paris*: Calmann-Lévy.
36   Schnapper, D. (1998) *Community of Citizenship: On the Modern Idea of Nationality*, London: Transaction Publishers.
37   The quotation is the title of Tilly, C. (1984) *Big Questions, Large Processes, Huge Comparisons*, New York: Russell Page Foundation.
38   Angell, N. and others (1933) *The Intelligent Man's Way to Avoid War*, London: Heinemann.
39   For example, Doob, L. (1964) *Patriotism and Nationalism: Their Psychological Foundations*, New Haven: Yale University Press.
40   Durkheim, E. (1992) *Leçons de Sociologie*, trans. by C. Brookfield, London: Routledge.

Further reading

GENERAL WORKS

Anderson, B. (1983) *Imagined Communities: Reflections on the Rise and Spread of Nationalism*, London: Verso.

This is the most quoted and perhaps the most influential recent work on nationalism.

Armstrong, J. A. (1982) *Nations before Nationalism*, Chapel Hill: University of North Carolina Press.

Addresses the historical puzzle about whether nations as currently understood existed before the invention of nationalist ideology in the late eighteenth and nineteenth centuries.

Deutsch, K. (1953, 1966) *Nationalism and Social Communication: An Enquiry into the Foundations of Nationality*, Cambridge (Mass.): MIT Press.

Propounds the argument that nations are established because of the intensity of communications between members of certain populations.

Gellner, E. (1983) *Nations and Nationalism*, Oxford: Blackwell.
— (1997) *Nationalism*, London: Weidenfeld & Nicolson.

Clearly and concisely explains the contention that nationalism is an essential element of modernity.

Hobsbawm, E. J. (1990) *Nations and Nationalism since 1780: Programme, Myth, Reality*, Cambridge: Cambridge University Press.

Is an historical account in the Marxist tradition which argues that nationalism is a dying phenomenon.

Nairn, T. (1997) *Faces of Nationalism: Janus Revisited*, London: Verso.

A stimulating, wide-ranging, and radical view of nationalism.

Billig, M. (1995) *Banal Nationalism*, London: Sage.

An original approach to nationalism showing the 'flagging' of the nation in everyday life.

Smith, A. D. (1986) *The Ethnic Origins of Nations*, Oxford: Blackwell.
—— (1995) *Nations and Nationalism in the Global Era*, Cambridge: Polity.

The most prolific work on nationalism, always worth reading.

Hedetoft, U. (1995) *Signs of Nations: Studies in the Political Semiotics of Self and Other in Contemporary European Nationalism*, Aldershot: Dartmouth.

An impressive theoretical and empirical study (although it is complex and difficult) of what the nation means for the British, Germans and Danes.

CHAPTER 1: THE COLD WAR AND NATIONALISM

LaFeber, W. (1997) *America, Russia and the Cold War, 1945–1996*, New York: Magraw-Hill.

Although the literature on the Cold War does not address the questions of super-power nationalism directly, this is a classic textbook is.

Hunter, A. (ed.) (1998) *Re-Thinking the Cold War*, Philadelphia: Temple.

Is also worth consulting.

CHAPTER 2: NATIONALISM AND MINORITIES

Caplin, R., Feffer, J. (eds.) (1996) *Europe's New Nationalism: States and Minorities in Conflict*, Oxford: Oxford University Press.
Ishiyame, J. T., Breunig, M. (1998) *Ethnopolitics and the New Europe*, London: Lynne Reiner.
Keating, M. (1988) *State and Regional Nationalism: Territorial Politics and the European State*, Brighton: Harvester Wheatsheaf.
Macdonald, S. (ed.) (1993) *Inside European Identities*, Berg: Oxford.

Heiberg, M. (1989) *The Making of the Basque Nation*, Cambridge: Cambridge University Press.
McCrone, D. (1992) *Understanding Scotland: The Sociology of a Stateless Nation*, London: Routledge.

Some of the best studies of small-nation nationalism are focused on particular cases. The last two titles listed are examples.

CHAPTER 3: EUROPEAN INTEGRATION AND GLOBALISATION

Amin, S. (1997) *Capitalism in the Age of Globalization*, London and New Jersey: Zed.
Laffan, B. (1996) 'The Politics of Identity and Political Order in Europe' *Journal of Common Market Studies*, 31, 1, 81–102.
Gray, J. (1998) *False Dawn: The Delusion of Global Capitalism*, London: Granta.
Nelson, R., Roberts, D., Veit, W. (eds.) (1992) *The Idea of Europe: Problems of Transnational Identity*, Oxford: Berg.
Wintle, M. (ed.) (1996) *Culture and Identity in Europe*, Avebury: Dartmouth.
Zetterholm, S. (ed.) (1994) *National Cultures and European Integration*, Oxford: Berg.

In an extensive literature, the works listed above are particularly relevant to this chapter.

CHAPTER 4: NATIONALISM AND IMMIGRATION

Baumgartl, B., Favell, A. (eds.) (1995) *New Xenophobia in Europe*, London, The Hague: Kluwer Law International.
Dummett A., Nicol, A. (1990) *Subjects, Citizens, Aliens and Others: Nationality and Immigration Law*, London: Weidenfield and Nicolson.
Brubaker, W. R. (1992) *Citizenship and Nationhood in France and Germany*, London: Harvard University Press.
Cornelius W. A., Martin, P. L., Hollifield, J. F., (eds.) (1994) *Controlling Immigration*, Stanford: Stanford University Press.
Noiriel, G. (1996) *The French Melting Pot: Immigration, Citizenship and National Identity*, Minneapolis: University of Minnesota Press.

There is an enormous literature on immigration. These are among the best studies.

CHAPTER 5: NATIONALISM AND THE BREAK-UP OF THE SOVIET UNION AND YUGOSLAVIA

Connor, W. (1984) *The National Question in Marxist-Leninist Theory and Strategy*, Princeton: Princeton University Press.

Danber, R. (1992) *The Soviet Nationality Reader: The Disintegration in Context*, Boulder: Westview.

Suny, R. G. (1993) *The Revenge of the Past: Nationalism, Revolution and the Collapse of the Soviet Union*, Stanford: Stanford University Press.

Woodward, L. S. (1995) *Balkan Tragedy: Chaos and Dissolution after the Cold War*, Washington: Brookings Institution.

CHAPTER 6: IRREDENTISM AND SEPARATISM

Anderson, M. (1996) *Frontiers: Territory and State Formation in the Modern World*, Cambridge: Polity Press.

Buccheit, L. C. (1978) *Secession: The Legitimacy of Self-Determination*, New Haven: Yale University Press.

Freeman, M. (1996) 'Democracy and Dynamite: The Peoples' Right to Self-Determination' *Political Studies* 44, 4, 746–61.

Cassese, A. (1996) *The Self-Determination of Peoples*, Cambridge: Cambridge University Press.

CHAPTER 7: DEMOCRACY AND NATIONALISM

Miller, D. (1995) *On Nationality*, Oxford: Clarendon Press.

Schnapper, D. (1998) *Community of Citizenship: on the Modern Idea of Nationality*, London: Transaction Publishers.

Tamir, Y. (1993) *Liberal Democracy*, Princeton: Princeton University Press.

The link between nationality, citizenship and democracy is explored in sections of these three important books.

MacCormick, N. (1994) 'What Place for Democracy in the Modern World' *Hume Papers on Public Policy*, 2, 1, Edinburgh: University of Edinburgh Press.

— (1996) 'Liberalism, Nationalism and the Post-Sovereign State' *Political Studies*, 44, 4, 553–67.

Neil MacCormick has a good claim to be the first in the field in the current debate on liberal nationalism, but unfortunately his writings are scattered.

Index